HISTORIC VIRGINIA

A Tour of More Than 75 of the State's Top National Landmarks

Laura A. Macaluso

Globe
Pequot

Guilford, Connecticut

With heartfelt thanks to Jeffrey and Klaus, my companions on many of these site visits across the Commonwealth of Virginia. There are a lot of miles—and even some paddling—on those tiny paws!

Globe
Pequot

An imprint of The Rowman & Littlefield Publishing Group, Inc.
4501 Forbes Blvd., Ste. 200
Lanham, MD 20706
www.rowman.com

Distributed by NATIONAL BOOK NETWORK

British Library Cataloguing in Publication Information available

Library of Congress Cataloging-in-Publication Data available

ISBN 978-1-4930-4183-1 (paperback)
ISBN 978-1-4930-4184-8 (e-book)

♾™ The paper used in this publication meets the minimum requirements of American National Standard for Information Sciences—Permanence of Paper for Printed Library Materials, ANSI/NISO Z39.48-1992.

CONTENTS

CHESAPEAKE BAY

COASTAL VIRGINIA

HEART OF APPALACHIA

NORTHERN VIRGINIA

SHENANDOAH VALLEY

INTRODUCTION

On my return to Fredericksburg, I walked through the house and opening the back door, looked down the hill across the fields and the river. The beauty of Virginia made me wonder how I could ever have left it even for a winter.

GARI MELCHERS, *NEW YORK HERALD TRIBUNE*, 1928

Virginia is geographically divided into 10 tourism regions based on the differing physical characteristics of the landscape. They are the Blue Ridge Highlands, Central Virginia, Chesapeake Bay, Coastal Virginia, Coast Virginia–Eastern Shore, Northern Virginia, Shenandoah Valley, Southwest Virginia, Southern Virginia Highlands, and the Virginia Mountains. Locals have developed cultural identities with different names tied to place, including Northern Virginia (called "NoVa" in Virginia parlance), Richmond (the capital city, often referred to as "RVA"), Tidewater (which includes the Northern Neck and Hampton Roads), and Southwest Virginia (SWVA for short). Further dicing up the state are the 95 counties and 39 independent cities that cover 42,775 square miles. The Commonwealth of Virginia is home to almost 8.5 million people and a bounty of flora and fauna that keeps naturalists, both amateur and professional, busy year-round.

Looking at the state's natural and cultural assets has been a project for Virginians since at least the era of Thomas Jefferson—a Founding Father, yes, but also the author of *Notes on the State of Virginia* (1783). This book—the only one he wrote and published—is a catalog of the state's natural and man-made assets, alongside some less favorable commentary on Jefferson's own perceptions of African Americans and Native Americans. Jefferson's deep interest in place continues right up to today, espoused in the award-winning tourism campaign "Virginia is for Lovers," which has been running successfully since 1969. For many years a feature of this campaign has incorporated public art: LOVE signs are spread around the state, from the southwest corner beyond the mountains to the northeast Chesapeake Bay, offer picturesque picture-taking places and reinforcing Virginia's many-headed tourism opportunities. "Virginia is for Lovers" reshapes itself to become "Virginia is for History Lovers," "Virginia is for Dog Lovers," "Virginia is for Mountain Lovers," "Virginia is for Beach Lovers," and so on.

In between 18th-century Thomas Jefferson and 20th-century "Virginia is for Lovers" are 200-plus years of celebrating a unique place, with a unique history. While that sentence might be true for any one of the 50 that make up these United States, if you were to look at the typical souvenir plate pictured here, there is of a mix of nature and culture that cannot be found anywhere else but Virginia, including examples of early history such as Jamestown, the first permanent English settlement in North America, and the Governor's Palace at the re-created but always beloved Williamsburg. Then there are the mythic and today sometimes troubled Founding Fathers and their houses Mount Vernon, Monticello, and Montpelier. Revolutionary War history is here at Yorktown, but so is the tomb of Stonewall Jackson in Lexington (where visitors sometimes still leave lemons) and Appomattox, the "place where the nation reunited," closing out the bloodiest four years in American history. And, part and parcel of this celebratory stance of the Old Dominion (another name for Virginia) are the natural features of the landscape, caverns such as Luray in the Shenandoah Valley, Natural Bridge in the Blue Ridge Mountains, and Virginia Beach, where the Chesapeake meets the Atlantic—a bit less "natural" than the others perhaps, but, beyond the souvenir shops and restaurants, it is still the favored place for Virginians to access large expanses of sand and rolling waves, while collecting seashells and watching shorebirds.

Some of the places painted onto the souvenir plate are National Historic Landmark sites, while others are not. According to the secretary of the interior, under which the National Park Service functions, and the administrator of the National Historic Landmarks (NHL) program, these are historic places that hold national significance. In other words, only select cultural and natural places receive such designation because of their ability to illustrate American history and heritage in the built or natural environment in a singular way. Today there are almost 2,600 National Historic Landmarks across the US. Some landmarks sit within National Register of Historic Places districts, while others stand alone. Some National Historic Landmarks are designated historic districts themselves.

Out of the 121 possible choices in Virginia, I've selected more than 75. The buildings and places that have National Historic Landmark designation are primarily dedicated to famous men, such as presidents Tyler, Wilson, and Ford; Civil War battlefields; Colonial Virginia and Revolutionary War figures such as George Washington, Patrick Henry, George Mason, Richard Henry Lee, James Madison, and Thomas Jefferson; historic churches, taverns, plantations, and manor houses; and military installations, docks, and ships. There are only a few National Historic Landmark designations for people of color, and only one dedicated to a woman. One

site associated with an artist makes the register—Gari Melchers, whose quote opens this introduction—while only one listing represents the earliest inhabitants of Virginia: the prehistoric Native American cultures that inhabited the land. Today their descendants consist of seven federally recognized tribes.

Although there are problems with the current list of National Historic Landmarks in Virginia, seeking out these sites will bring visitors and travelers into direct contact with a state that retains much of its agricultural heritage, with a heavy dose of myth-making around famous men that has created a specific identity for the state. There are many wondrous things to see in Virginia, and many wonderful places. Many of them are networked into trails, such as the Captain John Smith Chesapeake National Historic Trail, the Crooked Road, Road to Revolution Heritage Trail, and the Jefferson Heritage Trail. Creating your own National Historic Landmark trail is quite possible in the groupings of places I have outlined in this book. Pound the pavement (or dirt trail) with your feet or wheels and see history firsthand. You'll be rewarded with incredible natural vistas, exemplary architecture, defining historical events, and complex, inspiring people whose ideas have quite literally shaped the world we live in today.

Virginia dedicates her shrines, together with her recreational and scenic attractions in the mountains and by the sea and her intriguing natural wonders to the people of the nation. She bids one and all to come and share her glorious heritage with her people.

FROM THE CIRCA EARLY 1940S GUIDEBOOK, *CARRY ME BACK TO OLD VIRGINIA* PUBLISHED BY THE VIRGINIA CONSERVATION COMMISSION

Tobacco plants in a field.

Reynolds Homestead
(also known as Rock Spring Plantation)
463 Homestead Ln., Critz; (276) 694-7181; https://www.reynolds
homestead.vt.edu/; admission; house tours available weekends,
Apr through Oct 1 p.m. to 4 p.m.

Virginia is a state shaped by the tobacco industry, a product that was the economic impetus for English settlement in the 17th century. Even today the Tobacco Region Revitalization Commission exists to serve the tobacco-dependent communities that are still working to recover economically after the fall of "Big Tobacco" in the 1990s. Here at the Reynolds Homestead the story of one of the tobacco industry's 20th-century titans is told. The plantation was the birthplace and boyhood home of R. J. Reynolds who would found the R. J. Reynolds Tobacco Company and produce iconic brands such as Camel cigarettes. Designated a National Historic Landmark in 1977, the house and site are today managed by Virginia Tech's Office of Outreach and International Affairs as a continuing education and regional cultural center for the university and the community.

Rock Spring Plantation (the name of the Reynolds Homestead) was first developed in the early 19th century, when Abraham Reynolds built a log cabin on-site (no longer extant). His son developed the plantation landscape, erected the two-story brick Federal-style home with hipped roof in the years 1843 to 1855, and raised a family of 19 children, including Richard Joshua, or R. J., who lived here until he was 24. Outside of the house proper is the Reynolds family cemetery, but it is not the only cemetery on-site. Like many Virginia plantation houses, the enslaved population often lived and worked in close proximity to the owners, but were buried in their own cemeteries far from the plantation house. Virginia Tech, the current managers of the property, are working to document the biographies and lives of some of the people enslaved here at the Reynolds Homestead, including Kitty Reynolds. Kitty exemplifies the complex, close relationship that some enslaved people had to their enslavers. Born on a nearby plantation, Kitty married Anthony Reynolds, a man enslaved at the Rock Spring Plantation. Coming to Rock Spring Plantation, Kitty served the Reynolds family in multiple ways—as a midwife and child caretaker—but even after Emancipation, she remained in close contact with the Reynolds family. Although her portrait hangs in the kitchen, the difficulties in documenting the genealogies of enslaved people is seen in the cemetery here—fieldstones, often without inscriptions, mark gravesites. Some burials have no markings aboveground at all. The work can take years and decades, but most historic plantation sites in Virginia are engaged in this effort, from Monticello to Montpelier and many others including the Reynolds Homestead and even colleges such as the University of Virginia and Sweet Briar College.

The Reynolds house and remaining outbuildings have been restored, including a brick milk house, a log icehouse, a log granary, and a reconstructed tobacco barn. When R. J. was growing up here, there was also a store and a tobacco factory, but both are gone.

Monument Avenue Historic District,
see entry on p. 25.

CENTRAL VIRGINIA

Camp Rapidan (Camp Hoover)
Shenandoah National Park, Syria; nps.gov/shen/learn/history culture/rapidancamp.htm; special tours offered during late spring to fall via the National Park Service; free admission

One million visitors travel Skyline Drive every year—an example of a well-loved and well-known National Historic Landmark, located in Shenandoah National Park. But, unknown to most visitors, there is a second National Historic Landmark within the boundaries of Shenandoah that affords a unique look at the life of Depression-era president, Herbert Hoover.

During the 1920s, the US Congress began identifying large swaths of land east of the Mississippi in order to create new national parks that would match the grandeur of the earliest parks out west. Congress established the first and second national parks east of the Mississippi in 1926: the Great Smoky Mountains in Tennessee and North Carolina and Shenandoah in Virginia. According to the National Park Service: "In 1929, President Hoover built a rustic getaway on a trout stream high up in Madison County, inside the park's boundary, introducing many influential visitors to the pleasures of the Blue Ridge." When Hoover left office four years later in 1933,

he donated the camp to the people of the US, through the administration of the National Park Service.

Virginia is the home to seven American presidents—more than any other state in the Union—but it was also the summer retreat home of Herbert Hoover, the 31st US president. Born in Iowa, Hoover intended Camp Rapidan as a summer getaway from the stresses and steamy heat of Washington, D.C., and the relentless work undertaken to try and alleviate the Great Depression. Although you can hike to the camp, it is a four-mile walk with stream crossings across the Mill Prong and Rapidan Rivers (with waterfalls), and therefore the National Park Service offers transportation and ranger-led tours of the camp during the warm weather season. Originally built by the US Marines, there were 13 buildings on-site, although only 3 remain. Hoover intended Camp Rapidan to become the "official" presidential retreat, but Franklin Delano Roosevelt, who disliked Hoover intensely, moved the retreat to Maryland, giving title to Camp David, which is still in use today.

Camp Rapidan features the president's cabin, the Brown House (in opposition to the White House), historically refurnished to its 1929 appearance. A recently completed exhibit, located in the historic Prime Minister's Cabin, offers visitors insight into the Hoovers' lives and their time at Rapidan Camp, as well as Herbert C. Hoover's Depression-era presidency. You can spend time on the large patio overlooking the river and have a snack if you've brought one. Reservations can be made up to six months in advance if you want to join a ranger-led and van tour. If not, and you want to walk, the check the website for information about open days to visit the interior and see the exhibits. The hike starts at mile marker 53 on Skyline Drive. Park in the Milam Gap lot, then cross the parkway. The trail, called Mill Prong–Camp Rapidan Trail, picks up on the other side of the crosswalk. You'll quickly come up to a park post and take a left to start the trail. Check in at the Harry F. Byrd Sr. Visitor Center at mile marker 51 on Skyline Drive for maps, snacks, restrooms, and needed supplies before your walk.

Carter Glass House
605 Clay St., Lynchburg; (434) 845-7301; possible to visit interior of house during business hours, Mon through Fri

In 1976 the US was deep in the spirit of celebrating the Bicentennial. Much of the buildup to this year included identifying historic assets, undertaking preservation work, and creating new educational activities around the founding of the country. All communities—small and large—wanted to be a part of this moment, including the small city of Lynchburg, Virginia. Founded on the banks of the James River in 1786, in the 19th century the town was a major access point for commercial activities, including shipping tobacco. Manufacturing became big business by the end of

the century, and the historic city core was built in a variety of architectural styles common to the Victorian age. Many of these buildings have recently been revived, restored, and revitalized, attracting residents and visitors to its hilly streets.

Integrated into this period of Central Virginia history is Carter Glass (1858–1946), a lifelong Lynchburger who held a number of influential political positions and who chose to live in the Court House Hill area, overlooking downtown. The house that became a National Historic Landmark in 1976 is actually only one of three house sites associated to Glass in Lynchburg, but it is the one he lived in for most of his adult life outside of his home and work in Washington, D.C. During his productive years working in state and federal government, Glass was a US congressman, senator, and treasury secretary. He is known for championing the Federal Reserve System and the Glass-Steagall Act, which limited banking activities, and likewise known for his antagonism toward Franklin Delano Roosevelt's New Deal act. He was also a segregationist and advocated removing the vote from African Americans during the odious period of American history known as Jim Crow. Despite this, in 1924, Glass was on the cover of *Time*.

The house Glass purchased in 1907 was already historic, as it was built in 1827 by John Mill, a lawyer and architect. The house features a hipped roof, classical detailing, and a portico (or porch) with Ionic columns. The house passed out of private ownership after Glass's death and was purchased by the St. Paul's Episcopal Church—the oldest Episcopal parish in the Hill City that today uses the house as its Parish Hall (or administrative offices). Glass was born in a house, also downtown, of which a Virginia Historical Marker exists close to Monument Terrace. In addition, the other house associated to Glass is called Montview, which is now part of Liberty University's campus and where the Rev. Jerry Falwell is buried. Although today located within Lynchburg city limits, at the time, Montview was located in Campbell County and was considered Glass's country house.

While Glass is remembered nationally for his work for the federal government and his long service (the list is too extensive to include here), locally he is also remembered for his contribution to the city's long-running newspaper, the *Lynchburg News*. Glass became a reporter and editor and eventually purchased other city newspapers, coalesced into one publication: the *Lynchburg News & Advance*, published to this day. Carter Glass Memorial Bridge over Route 29 from Lynchburg to Amherst is named for him. Another entry on the National Historic Landmark list, that of Robert Russa Moton High School, makes the perfect response to the deeply racist political and social views of Glass and of the *Lynchburg News & Advance*, which kept African Americans' photographs and news out of the paper until the Civil Rights movement of the 1960s.

Egyptian Building
1223 E. Marshall St., Richmond; maps.vcu.edu/mcv/egyptianbldg

Right around the corner, and in fact, abutting the rear of Monumental Church is one of the best examples of 19th-century Egyptian Revival architecture in the US. Surrounded by concrete and glass modern structures for the hospital and university that currently own and use the building, the imposing Egyptian-styled structure stands as a testament to the many sources of inspiration of the Victorian era. Americans of the 19th century weren't afraid to look far and wide for architectural sources and for

the decorative arts—they could pull from places as far afield as Old England, Italy, Morocco, or Egypt and design buildings that called upon ancient history, as applied in a New World setting. In this case the medical department at Hampden-Sydney College, later renamed the Medical College of Virginia (now part of Virginia Commonwealth University), chose the Egyptian Revival style to reflect the building's use as a space for medical education.

Egyptomania, the revival of interest in all things Egyptian, had occurred at the turn of the 19th century, after Napoleon invaded Egypt and rediscovered many ancient treasures, such as the Sphinx. Napoleon sponsored a scientific expedition, and a member of his army was deep in the work of deciphering the Rosetta Stone—the key to unlocking hieroglyphics. Images and ideas about Egypt spread throughout the West in the form of prints and books. Medical students were interested in Egypt, too, because the architect of the Great Pyramid at Giza, Imhotep, was also the world's first named physician. Egypt, therefore, gave rise to modern medicine in the Western world. The college's medical board chose Philadelphia architect Thomas Somerville Stewart for his Egyptian Revival design, which stands imposing on a small mound. The modern temple of learning opened in 1846.

If you study ancient Egyptian architecture in an art history survey class, you will find many elements brought together here. The building has deep porches, called porticos, on each side, with monumental columns within that are decorated with lotus capitals. The shafts of each of the columns are designed as bundles of reeds, which represent the Nile and its life-giving force. Reeds also signify papyrus, which is the plant material Egyptians used to write on after flattening, including for their *Book of the Dead*. Although the Egyptian Building was constructed of brick, it was covered in stucco in a sand color, which reminds viewers of the landscape of Egypt outside of the Nile delta, and of the sandstone blocks used to construct temples and pyramids. Below the structure at street level, the Egyptian Building is surrounded by fencing that ends with obelisks. The interior of the building is highly decorated with the symbols and colors of ancient Egypt.

This building, considered the oldest medical college building in the South, originally held medical lecture halls, a dissecting room, an infirmary, and hospital beds. Today it continues as classroom space for Virginia Commonwealth University.

Exchange Building
15 W. Bank St., Petersburg; (804) 835-9630; petersburg preservationtaskforce.com/museums/the-exchange-building; Thurs through Sat 10 a.m. to 4 p.m.; admission charged

Located on the Appomattox River, Petersburg is a historic city directly south of Richmond. Sometimes overlooked due to the richness of the state's heritage, Petersburg offers a full day or more of touring and sightseeing, especially for those with an interest in architectural history, African American history, and Civil War history. The city is surrounded by battlefield parks, but within city limits is Petersburg's Old Town, the oldest section of the city and a National Historic District containing more than 174 buildings of interest. Here you can find historic houses and churches from the 18th and 19th centuries, as well as a railroad depot, the Appomattox Iron Works, City Market, and the Exchange Building—these last structures part of the economic development of the city with regional impact.

The Exchange Building, the only National Historic Landmark in Petersburg, is a two-story, five-bay building with a hipped roof that served as a center for trade in the mid- to late-19th century, when tobacco and cotton were sold at auction. The Greek Revival design of the building, with its Doric order of columns on the portico (the Doric order is the earliest, simplest form of Greek architecture) under a pediment, must have provided a feeling of solidity and refinement to the messy practice of commodities trade—which here also included the sale of human beings. Conceived as a meeting place for merchants, the Exchange Building was designed by a New York architect. The building has open bays on both sides of the first floor, just as a temple to the Greek gods looked in Athens. Here the bays allowed access for goods for sale. There is also a central circular room under the dome. The Exchange Building has national significance due to its almost unaltered appearance, despite the fact that in the 20th century the building was used as a bank, as a police court, and for shops.

The success of Petersburg as a center for mercantile trade translated into the city becoming one of the major supply centers for the Confederate Army during the Civil War. For many years, the Exchange Building held the Siege Museum, a city-sponsored entity, where visitors learned about the longest siege in American history—the 10 long months of 1864 into 1865, when the Union Army pressed in on the Northern Army of Virginia in Richmond and Petersburg, ultimately forcing the Confederate Army to retreat west to Appomattox and surrender. But, in 2018, after a massive financial free fall for Petersburg, the city eliminated the Siege Museum from its municipal funding, and a group of volunteers called Petersburg Preservation gathered to create a new museum and visitor center in the Exchange Building, which would focus not just on Civil War history, but the history of Petersburg as a whole, from the Native American presence to today.

Five Forks Battlefield

9840 Courthouse Rd., Dinwiddie; (804) 732-3531; nps.gov/pete/ learn/historyculture/five-forks.htm; free admission; open 7 days a week 9 a.m. to 5 p.m.

The name Five Forks refers to the intersection of four roads at the site where one of the last battles of the Civil War took place on April 1, 1865. Today, overlooking these crossroads is a single cannon and a small monument with the National Historic

Landmark bronze plaque. The battle is part of the Siege on Richmond and Petersburg (see related entry, Petersburg Breakthrough Battlefield). The 37-mile line around Petersburg had been broken by the Union Army, when Lt. Gen. Ulysses S. Grant attacked Gen. Robert E. Lee's Northern Army of Virginia here at Five Forks, capturing the last functioning rail line into Petersburg, thus effectively cutting off the Confederate Army from supplies and the city's residents from the outside world. The siege was over and Lee ordered evacuation of both Richmond and Petersburg on April 2, the last strongholds of the Confederate Army in Virginia, and of the Confederacy itself.

These last desperate days of the long, appalling Civil War saw attempts by Lee to halt the progress of the Unionists. Lee ordered Major General George Pickett to "hold Five Forks at all hazards. Protect road to Ford's Depot and prevent Union forces from striking the Southside Railroad . . ." General Philip Sheridan led the Union Army here and had double the number of men in uniform. The Confederates dug in, hastily building defenses comprised of logs with dirt built up in front, along the White Oak Road. Sheridan led a cavalry charge, and the Confederate forces were overtaken. Sheridan knew, after 10 months of the stalemate, that the end was near, and he was ready for it, later saying, "I was exceedingly anxious to attack at once, for the sun was getting low, and we had to fight or go back . . ." Gen. George Custer was here, as was Robert E. Lee's son, Rooney. This battle, sometimes called the "Waterloo of the Civil War," pushed Lee and the Army of Northern Virginia farther west toward their fate at Appomattox Court House—the final campaign of the war—with Grant and the Union Army in close and constant pursuit.

Five Forks Battlefield is located in Dinwiddie County, a rural area of Central Virginia. Part of the battlefield site is a unit of Petersburg National Battlefield, with public access that includes access trails to points of interest in the area. An area of more than 1,200 acres around Five Forks was declared a National Historic Landmark in 1960. There is a visitor center on-site where you watch a short video, view museum exhibits, and pick up maps to follow the Five Forks Recreational Trail System. Out on the trails visitors see earthworks created by the Confederate Army as well as a cannon. For those with a deep interest in the final days of the Civil War, there are signs and accompanying interpretation from Richmond to Appomattox called "Lee's Retreat." See the detailed brochure, civilwartrails.org/docs/Lees-Retreat-brochure.pdf.

Jackson Ward Historic District
Forty city blocks contained between 4th St., Marshall St., Smith St., and the Richmond-Petersburg Tpke., Richmond; nps.gov/nr/travel/richmond/jacksonwardhd.html

Certainly as a designated area within Richmond, the Jackson Ward Historic District makes a good comparison to Monument Avenue (see Monument Avenue Historic District): Both are the only two neighborhoods in Richmond to have National Historic Landmark District status. The polarity of these two National Historic Landmarks is enlightening: Both exist in the same city, at the same time in history, with different people doing very different things. Seen against the monumentalizing of

the Confederacy happening on the west side of Richmond, here on the east side, African Americans of the early 20th century were establishing successful businesses and small-scale enterprises, called the Harlem of the South—basically a city within a city.

The name Jackson Ward came from the area's political polling district in Richmond, in use from 1871 to 1905, when the area was filled with immigrants, mainly Italian, Jewish, and German. As the area become predominantly black at the turn of the 20th century, the name continued to be associated with the area and was never changed. The architecture of Jackson Ward—called "visually cohesive"—is dominated by modest, three-bay townhouse structures in brick. Some have locally made cast-iron porches still intact, which are ornamental and reminiscent of garden structures. The most famous of all of these styled homes is that of Maggie Lena Walker, whose townhouse is now a unit of the National Park Service and open to the public (see Maggie Lena Walker House). The first African-American chartered bank opened here in 1886, and the area was thus also sometimes referred to as the "Black Wall Street." Everything within the area—fraternal organizations, banks, churches, schools, and insurance companies—was led by black owners, making this is unique, powerful place for African American community and culture. Included within the district today is the Black History Museum & Culture Center of Virginia (122 W. Leigh Street), which was originally a private mansion later turned into a public library for African Americans. The building is currently undergoing a full renovation

to become a more robust museum in which to tell the stories of the Jackson Ward Historic District, including the work of late-20th-century activists and local leaders who fought for desegregation and civil rights.

Culturally Jackson Ward was a center for entertainment and the enjoyment of vocal and musical talent. Performance venues included the Hippodrome Theater, which saw the 20th century's greatest talents: Duke Ellington, Ella Fitzgerald, Bill "Bojangles" Robinson (who has a monument at the intersection of Chamberlayne

Parkway, West Leight, and Adams Street), Lena Horne, Cab Calloway, Nat King Cole, and James Brown.

Like many communities in the mid-20th century, Jackson Ward ended up suffering from people relocating to the suburbs, redevelopment, and the construction of new highways, which was intended to drive economic development in urban areas, but very often decimated neighborhoods, businesses, and local culture. The role of the city council in redeveloping Jackson Ward was particularly cruel: In the 1950s thousands of black-owned houses were demolished to make way for public housing, destroying stability and sense of place. Today Jackson Ward, like many American communities, continues to work on rehabilitating their historic structures and bringing back small businesses and restaurants to sustain a local economy and local workforce. The Jackson Ward Historic District was placed on the National Register of Historic Places in 1976—the year Americans celebrated the Bicentennial.

James Madison's Montpelier
1350 Constitution Hwy., Montpelier Station; (540) 672-2728; montpelier.org; admission charged

Out in Orange County, on the aptly named Constitution Route, sits Montpelier, a house and what was once a working plantation, as all Virginia mansions were. James Madison (1751–1836) rebuilt his father's home on a small hill overlooking an expanse of agricultural fields and streams, with far distant views of the Blue Ridge Mountains. A born-and-bred aristocratic Virginian, Madison drafted the Constitution, the Federalist Papers, and the Bill of Rights, and he followed Thomas Jefferson

into service in the federal government, first as secretary of state and then as president. He married the beguiling socialite Dolley Payne Todd, who helped her husband to the White House. Today Montpelier retains 2,650 of the original acreage, and much effort has been spent in recent years in reestablishing the enslaved community story through new interpretation, the erection of buildings that would have served as houses and work spaces, and archaeology. Montpelier, like Monticello and Poplar Forest, works with the descendants of the enslaved and with scholars to bring to light forgotten or marginalized stories.

James Madison and Thomas Jefferson were great friends, sharing books, ideas, and much time together—one room in Monticello, Jefferson's primary house, was even named for Madison. Both men also shared a dependency on the institution of slavery, and both of their plantations were not profitable enough to ensure financial stability. Neither Madison nor Jefferson freed the majority of their slaves upon their death. Much of this lamentable history was lost after the Civil War and, in the case of Montpelier, was ignored when the house became, in the first part of the 20th century, a horse farm under the ownership of the William duPont family. Montpelier is unique in many ways: It is the only National Historic Landmark in this book owned by the National Trust for Historic Preservation. The house and land were given to the trust with an endowment, and the Montpelier Foundation manages the sites and oversees its daily work.

After visiting the interior of the brick Georgian house, be sure to visit the James Madison Landmark Forest. Accessible by trail, the forest has been intact since Madison's era. The house itself displays two distinct eras of ownership: that of James and Dolley Madison—who moved here at the end of the 18th century and adapted the house at least twice for their needs—and that of the duPont family, who did the same and remained in the house until 1984. Today, the duPont family's tenure is summed up by a visit to the art deco "Red Room" and when viewing the steeplechase outside, as well as the enclosed gardens nearby. There is a cafe on-site, and a variety of tours, based inside and outside of the main house, is offered daily. Finally, in an unusual addition to the story of slavery and its aftermath, visitors can see the Gilmore Cabin, a structure built by George Gilmore, once enslaved at Montpelier, who gained freedom at the end of the Civil War and built his family this home close to the entrance gates in 1873.

James Monroe Tomb
412 South Cherry St., Hollywood Cemetery, Richmond; (804) 648-8501; hollywoodcemetery.org; open daily 8 a.m. to 5 p.m.; free

In a state full of history, it seems strange that this tomb and this cemetery are the only ones of their type listed with National Historic Landmark status. But, wait, there are many more tombs in Virginia that are part of National Historic Landmark sites, including George Washington's tomb at Mount Vernon, Thomas Jefferson's grave at Monticello, and James Madison's gravesite at Montpelier. There's also Robert E. Lee's burial site within Lee Chapel on the campus of Washington & Lee. So, in fact, there are quite a few Founding Father gravesites—and James Monroe, being of that coterie, gets National Historic Landmark status, too. But Monroe's tomb is recognized in Hollywood Cemetery not just because it is his final resting place—after all, president and fellow Virginian John Tyler is buried at Hollywood, as well, but his tomb does not have landmark status. Monroe's tomb has landmark status because of the unusual and evocative Gothic Revival ironwork design erected upon his death in 1859.

So why isn't James Monroe, fifth US president, friend to Thomas Jefferson, and creator of the Monroe Doctrine buried at his primary homesite, which is called Highland and is in Charlottesville? Monroe and his wife Elizabeth lived at Highland until her death in 1830. After this, Monroe went to live with his daughter Maria in New York City, and he died there the following year on July 4. Monroe was buried in New York City's Marble Cemetery but was reinterred here in Richmond's Hollywood Cemetery in 1858—an indication that Southerners were beginning to agitate against the abolitionists and refocus their identities on their Southern heritage. Monroe, born in Westmoreland County, Virginia, needed to be brought back to Old Dominion.

Monroe's tomb, called the "birdcage" locally, sits in Presidents Circle, close to the tomb of John Tyler overlooking the James River. Albert Lybrock designed the architectural form using cast iron, a new material then being used to build facades on 19th-century commercial buildings in urban cities. His sarcophagus within is granite, while the openwork tracery (also called a grille), a style often used in medieval church architecture, is similar to Henry VII's tomb in Westminster Abbey. Lybrock was in fact, a European, having immigrated to the US in 1852 and settled in Richmond. The "birdcage" was painted black for decades, until the Department of General Services, spending tens of thousands of dollars, restored the cast-iron work and painted it ivory—the original color scheme—in 2015. Although the tomb seems an anomaly today, especially when viewed against the homogenous Virginia favored architectural style of Classicism, the style is recognizable for its time. The Victorian era around the Atlantic favored the Gothic for ecclesiastical and spiritual architecture (not to mention some domestic architecture, too), and since Hollywood Cemetery was designed in the rural garden style, the place was meant to evoke a charming garden in which to walk and enjoy the trees, plantings, and, yes, even the tomb architecture, which was considered closer to sculpture.

John Marshall House

818 E. Marshall St., Richmond; (804) 648-7998; preservation virginia.org/historic-sites/john-marshall-house; open Mar 1 through Dec 29, Fri and Sat 10 a.m. to 5 p.m., Sun noon to 5 p.m.; admission charged

John Marshall is a Founding Father from Virginia of a different sort. Although he wasn't the first chief justice of the US Supreme Court—he was the fourth—Marshall stayed in his position for 30 years, defining the role for his era, and ours. President John Adams appointed Marshall to the court in 1801, and it was from this house that Marshall left for Washington, D.C., although he spent much time at home working his cases and is believed to have written most of his opinions in this house. He was known in his own lifetime as the "Great Chief Justice," and he presided over cases establishing precedent that have lasted to this day. Marshall knew and was part of political tradition in Virginia and in early national politics, as he was the leader of the Federalist Party along with John Adams, against the Jeffersonian Republican tradition. Over the course of his work life, Chief Justice Marshall participated in more than 1,000 cases, some of them, such as *Marbury v. Madison* (1803), establishing the power of the judicial branch of government. Most famously, Marshall presided over the trial of Aaron Burr, who had shot and killed Alexander Hamilton in a duel. Burr was acquitted of all charges.

John Marshall and his wife Mary Ambler Marshall (known as Polly) built the house in the up-and-coming fashionable Court End District of Richmond in 1790. A modest Federal-style house in brick, there are interior hand-carved decorations in wood throughout the domestic spaces. Marshall kept assiduous records of the house construction, including the names of the builders. Marshall's property, originally the size of the whole city lot, included a two-story law office, a stable, and detached buildings for service work such as cooking and laundry. The original landscape must have offered Marshall and his family a sense of rural life in the city: There was a small orchard, gardens, and even a brook running through the property. Over time pieces of the land were sold as the neighborhood and city grew, leaving the Marshall House on a small plot of land.

As with many of the National Historic Landmark sites in this book, the John Marshall House, was slated for demolition before being saved by an interested local group of advocates. Today the house is managed by Preservation Virginia, which offers a 45-minute tour with an interpreter or a self-guided tour. Special small exhibits offer a look into current court cases and judicial topics through artwork. Around the house replanted historic Virginia flower gardens and plantings, including holly, southern magnolia, elm, mulberry, and willow oak, help re-create a sense of the landscape of the 19th century. John Marshall, called a "giant of the American judiciary system," deserves to be better known in American memory. Another Richmond-based group, the John Marshall Foundation, is working to do just that.

Maggie Lena Walker House (Maggie L. Walker Historic Site)
600 N. Second St., Richmond; (804) 771-2017; nps.gov/mawa/ index.htm; open year-round for tours, check website for details; free

Located within the Jackson Ward Historic District, the home of Maggie Lena Walker became part of the National Park Service in 1978. Walker, an African-American woman, the daughter of a former slave, who eventually had to use a wheelchair, was one of the backbone entrepreneurs of the neighborhood, helping to shape its identity as a center for business, culture, and opportunity for black residents of Richmond and beyond. She was, in fact, the first American woman to lead a bank at a time when women, and especially women of color, were doing no such thing. She was a force of nature, driven by her Christian faith and commitment to her family and community.

When Walker, her husband Armstead, and their sons moved to the Jackson Ward District in 1905, Walker became involved with all things related to church, community, and entrepreneurship. She had already chartered the St. Luke Penny Savings Bank, convincing her African-American neighbors that they needed a banking institution that worked for them, helping to build financial stability and generational wealth. Walker was the founder and the first president of the bank, a role that would prove even more important when her husband was accidentally killed in 1915. The bank, at First and Marshall Streets, was designed by Charles R. Russell and featured an elegant Italianate Revival redesign of the Gilded Age, complete with rich interiors of finely carved woodwork and tiled floors. The bank was in business for more than 100 years, always remembering Walker's mission that, "the bank will take . . . nickels and turn them into dollars."

Jackson Ward Historic District, the "city within a city," had a growth of middle-income individuals and families in the early 20th century. Walker lived here with hospital staff, barbers, grocers, shop owners, insurance agents, and teachers. The housing built to accommodate residents were most often long streets of attached townhouses, as Walker's surviving townhouse, turned museum, attests. Walker lived on East Leigh Street, which was called "Quality Row" for the established individuals who lived there. Walker's house, today identifiable by its green-and-white striped awnings, was built and then rebuilt in successive stages over the course of decades. Walker's sons and grandchildren lived with her, necessitating that extra rooms be added onto the structure, while an elevator and other amenities became necessary in 1928, when she became confined to a wheelchair due to frail health.

MAGGIE LENA WALKER

Walker lived until 1934 and was recognized nationally after her death. The house stayed in the family until 1979, when the National Park Service purchased it and all of its contents, enabling the house to be interpreted true to Walker's life as she lived it. A 10-foot-tall bronze monument to Walker was installed and dedicated in Richmond in 2017, serving as the gateway to the Jackson Ward Historic District.

Main Street Station and Trainshed
1500 E. Main St., Richmond; (804) 646-6246; mainstreetstation richmond.com; open daily year-round; free

Richmond's Main Street Station and Trainshed is the only train station to be listed as a National Historic Landmark in Virginia, and its rise and fall and rise again follows the history of American transportation and society. Built in the 1890s, when cities were flush with cash and grand architectural designs for better living, the train was the preferred mode of transportation for Gilded Age well-to-do Americans, as it was the era directly before the first cars became available. Richmond wanted a statement building as its "gateway," and the Chesapeake & Ohio and Seaboard Air Line railroads chose a large-scale Beaux-Arts design with emphasis on a Romanesque

architectural heritage for this signature building. At the time of its design, the work was contemporary with aesthetic taste. But a halt in work of 10 years in the first decade of the 20th century meant that by the time the building was online and servicing trains, the architecture was already out of date, looking a bit old-fashioned compared to New York's Grand Central Terminal, for example, built in the Beaux-Arts style.

Behind the station proper is a 530-foot-long train shed, just one of seven such covered buildings in the nation. Here trains would pull in and cover passengers from the elements. This kind of functional design is well-known in Europe (think King's Cross Station in England or the Gare du Nord in Paris). The firm of Wilson, Harrison, and Richards from Philadelphia, who also designed the Reading Terminal, was chosen for the design work. The project cost in the millions, little today compared to monies spent in refurbishing the site at the turn of the 21st century. The Main Street Terminal and Trainshed were heavily used until the early 1970s, as transportation options and American consumer tastes changed significantly. Then, a series of urban issues around the location in Shockoe Bottom—a traditionally African-American neighborhood in Richmond—including flooding, hit the area hard. Finally, I-95 was built directly around the Main Street Terminal and Trainshed, a sign that train travel had been eclipsed by the automobile. All of these factors led to the further decline of the building and its environment. The last Amtrak train left the Main

Street Station in 1975, and a year later a fire on the platform caused great damage. The station was in danger of demolition.

Fortunately, developers saw opportunity in the all-but-abandoned Main Street Station building. Unfortunately, they tried a tactic that at the time had worked for other American cities such as Philadelphia and Washington, D.C.: The station was turned into a mall. This failed rather quickly, but it had staved off any question of demolition. In the meantime, small business owners were coming back to the area and opening restaurants and shops. In addition, the federal government had instituted a series of programs to address the ill effects of pollution caused by the hundreds of thousands cars that pass through Richmond on the highway system. City leaders wanted people to stay in the capital city—not drive through it. The revival of the Main Street Station began. Today the area is bustling, and though challenges remain to train service, Amtrak is a success in Virginia, and the Main Street Station and Trainshed in Richmond, after millions of dollars spent on renovations and in train service, is once again a welcome gateway to the capital city.

Monument Avenue Historic District
Monument Ave. from the 1200 block of W. Franklin to the intersection of Monument and Roseneath Rds., Richmond; nps.gov/nr/Travel/richmond/MonumentAveHD.html; open 24/7 year-round

Monuments come up, and monuments come down, and they have been a source of controversy through the ages. There is no better place to look at the current controversies around monument culture than in Richmond, along Monument Avenue, a City Beautiful–styled planned residential neighborhood decorated with some of the largest bronze monuments to the heroes of the Confederacy and the South. Along this green boulevard are large and small houses in a plethora of Gilded Age architectural styles, built on both sides of the wide paved streets. In the median strips—large enough for walking the dog, but not for public parks—overscaled equestrian bronzes, granite plinths, and marble statuary appear, the largest works of art in the public sphere in the city.

The Robert E. Lee Monument is the center of it all, in a sense, because he was painted from the very beginning as the hero of the South and the Confederate cause. At more than 60 feet tall, his monument is the largest and had the largest dedication event on May 28, 1890—100,000 people were drawn here, including very old veterans of the Civil War, who sat around the base and watched the crowds span out before them. The Lee Monument was later joined by monuments to Thomas "Stonewall" Jackson, Jefferson Davis, J. E. B. Stuart, Matthew Fontaine Maury, and much later, in 1996, Arthur Ashe. The placement and design of the Ashe Monument was controversial and a sign of things to come—all of the other statues were of white

men linked directly to the Confederacy. Ashe was an African-American tennis star and humanitarian. Reconciling this information isn't easy.

The question about the current status of these Monument Avenue monuments is this: Should the 21st century keep these monuments in place, as is, knowing many of them were created during the days of Jim Crow—that is legalized, economic, and social repression of African Americans—or should these monuments be removed, or somehow altered, to include the full story of their origin and meaning? Scholars argue that such monumental works serve to keep white supremacy fresh and that continuing right up to today, these types of public artworks are more harmful than positive, affecting people and their place in society. To this end, Virginia cities such as Charlottesville and Richmond have sought to address the social ills caused by monuments, commissioning studies to document and examine the full impact of the histories and ideas presented in these monuments. The Commonwealth of Virginia has in place a law that states that war memorials cannot be removed, and in late 2018 this law was cited as the reason that the city could not remove any of the monuments, even that of Jefferson Davis, arguably the easiest one to pull from the group, since Davis was not a war veteran but a political leader. These concerns and questions about monuments won't be going anyway anytime soon. Virginia has the most monuments to the Confederacy in the country, and Monument Avenue is the epitome of that movement, called the "Lost Cause."

Monumental Church
**1224 E. Broad St., Richmond; (804) 643-7407; historicrichmond
.com/property/monumental-church; open select days of the year**

Located in the Court End Historic District in the capital city, Monumental Church is monumental, but the idea of a "monument" in this case has more to do with the origin of the Latin word *monere*, which means "a coming to mind." In other words,

Monumental Church was built to remember an event. In this case, this church is a monument to the 72 people who died in a theater fire on this site on December 26, 1811. That it was the day after Christmas, that so many people died so horribly, and that it happened in a small city such as Richmond meant that the event impacted people enormously, causing a group to come together and commission the design and erection of a Christian church that also acted as a memorial site for the dead. This makes this church unique, but the architectural form created by Robert Mills reflects the dual purpose: Mills's design uses both Greek and Egyptian architectural features, fusing together the ancient world idea of everlasting life to that of contemporary Christian beliefs.

Chief Justice John Marshall (whose house is a National Historic Landmark, described in a separate entry) headed the committee that began speaking with America's earliest professional architects: Benjamin Henry Latrobe and Robert M. Mills. In the end, after some professional squabbling, Mills, America's first native-born professional architect and a student of Thomas Jefferson, was chosen for the work based on his unique design that fit the bill of being both a church and a monument to the dead: the building is an octagon capped with a dome (a Jeffersonian trait—see the Monticello entry). The monument under the front portico, which is enlarged and which Mills himself called "emphatic," is inscribed with the names of the dead near a large urn. This detail connects Monumental Church to the history of the ancient world and religious beliefs: the ancient Egyptians, Greeks, Romans, and many others decorated urns for use at cemeteries. Below the church is a crypt located beneath the sanctuary that contains the remains of those who died in the fire. Although the building's architectural mix derives from Europe, the building material is all Virginia: Aquia Creek sandstone covered in stucco.

Monumental Church was built on the theater site that previously had contained a timber-framed large building that saw action not only as a theater, but also where the Virginia Ratifying Convention of 1788—including Thomas Jefferson, James Madison, James Monroe, and John Marshall—met for three weeks. The church was therefore built on historical events that shaped the people of Richmond. For example, in 1817 Monumental Church established the first Sunday School program in Richmond, while many famous parishioners called Monument Church their home parish, including Chief Justice John Marshall; Edgar Allan Poe, whose foster parents, the Allans, were members; and the Marquis de Lafayette when he visited Richmond in 1824. Monumental Church served as an Episcopal church until 1965, when it was deconsecrated. The National Historic Landmark is now owned by Historic Richmond, a not-for-profit organization that opens the building for visitors and private functions.

Petersburg Breakthrough Battlefield (part of Pamplin Historical Park & the National Museum of the Civil War Soldier)

6125 Boydton Plank Rd., Pamplin Historical Park & the National Museum of the Civil War Soldier, Petersburg; (877) 726-7546; pamplinpark.org/things-to-do/petersburg-breakthrough-battlefield; open Mar through Nov, daily 9 a.m. to 5 p.m., weekends only Dec through Feb; admission charged

The Siege of Petersburg is part of a long and complex story focused on the last year of the Civil War, which is represented in several historic areas in and around Petersburg, including the Exchange Building (see separate entry) and Petersburg Breakthrough Battlefield, a National Historic Landmark District, which is embedded in a privately run not-for-profit organization called Pamplin Historical Park and the National Museum of the Civil War Soldier. All of these are tied to the story interpreted and managed by the National Park Service at Petersburg National Battlefield and to the Five Forks Battlefield site (see separate entry).

Petersburg Breakthrough Battlefield is the location of the Third Battle of Petersburg, where the Union Army finally broke through Confederate lines on April 2, 1865, after a 10-month-long siege. Protecting Richmond and Petersburg—the capital of the Confederacy and its supply center—was of paramount importance to Gen. Robert E. Lee. The Union Army knew this, too, and under direction from Lt. Gen. Ulysses S. Grant, there was one goal: to gain control of Richmond and capture the Confederate Army. There are several ways to understand this long battle, including

partaking in two driving tours of the Eastern front and the Western front in and around Petersburg and walking the grounds at Pamplin Historical Park, which contains the most intact Confederate Army earthworks anywhere—more than 1,700 linear feet of them, snaking through the landscape as reminders of the thousands of men who lived here through a winter and a seemingly unending siege.

Within Pamplin Historical Park & the National Museum of the Civil War Soldier is a 424-acre historical campus that includes museums, antebellum homes, the Petersburg Breakthrough Battlefield, and a slave life exhibit. The founders of the museum managed to make several purchases of this land in Dinwiddie County beginning in the 1990s. The land would likely have become residential and commercial development otherwise. Currently the largest privately owned Civil War museum in the country, Pamplin Historical Park continues to acquire and develop Civil War–related objects such as the Banks House, which was used as Gen. Grant's headquarters. In addition to the exhibits and earthworks, the National Historic Landmark site contains archaeological evidence of Confederate camps, rifle pits (also known as foxholes), two military dams, and a large redan—which is an arrow-shaped fortification, although here it appears as a moon-shaped crescent on a 15-foot artificial mound—which was built for viewing troop movement. There are also re-creations of log cabins and the Hart House, an antebellum house located within the district and the scene of fighting in both October 1864 and April 1865.

Robert Russa Moton High School (Robert Russa Moton Museum)
900 Griffin Blvd., Farmville; (434) 315-8775; motonmuseum.org; call for hours; admission charged

Known today as the Robert Russa Moton Museum, this building—once a rural high school located in Prince Edward County—is called the "birthplace of the student civil rights movement." And no wonder! On April 23, 1951, 16-year-old student Barbara Rose Johns led a strike at her school to protest unequal conditions for African-American students. Her idealism, planning, and persistence ultimately garnered the support of National Association for the Advancement of Colored People (NAACP) attorneys Spotswood Robinson and Oliver Hill. After meeting with the students and the community, Robinson and Hill filed suit at the federal courthouse in Richmond, Virginia. The case, *Davis v. Prince Edward*, became one of five that the US Supreme Court decided on May 17, 1954, in *Brown v. Board of Education*. From this momentous ruling it was determined by the Supreme Court that segregation was unconstitutional, a decision that changed not only America, but the world.

Part of the US Civil Rights Trail (civilrightstrail.com), comprised of 100 sites across 14 states, the Moton Museum today welcomes all visitors to learn about the fight for equality that lasted for more than a decade and involved people of all ages, colors, and creeds. The focus of the museum is the history of the people who used the building, which began life in 1939 as a segregated and overcrowded high school. Although designed in a refined Classical Revival style in red brick, traditional of Virginia architecture, conditions were always less favorable than the atmosphere at publicly funded white schools, and eventually overcrowding meant the erection of shabbily constructed tar shacks to house more students. Barbara Johns and fellow students staged a walkout, which precipitated the legal

challenges, but even *Brown v. Board of Education* didn't stop segregation in Virginia.

It is hard to believe today, but in the years 1959 to 1964, the State of Virginia allowed some counties such as Prince Edward to close all public schools rather than fund integrated schools. During this time African-American students were forced to find other ways to continue their studies or move to another area, while white students enrolled in new so-called private schools that continued to receive state aid. Eventually, an integrated public school system was forced to reopen. Moton School remained in use until 1993, and then was finally shuttered, becoming a museum and then a National Historic Landmark in 1998. The school-turned-museum received a multimillion-dollar makeover, and today it runs school visits, programs, and tours in which visitors hear the voices of those involved in the strikes and learn of the long road to equality within the public education system.

A portrait of Barbara Rose Johns (later Powell) features a bright, composed student sitting at her school desk with hardcover books and a notebook ready for action. Louis Briel's portrait of Johns was unveiled at the Virginia Capitol—another National Historic Landmark (see separate entry)—on Constitution Day, September 17, 2010, and now hangs in the Moton Museum. In 2018 a bill was introduced in the House of Representative to award Johns a posthumous Congressional Gold Medal.

Sayler's Creek Battlefield (Sailor's Creek Battlefield State Park)
6541 Saylers Creek Rd., Rice; (804) 561-7510; dcr.virginia.gov/ state-parks/sailors-creek#general_information; open dawn to dusk; visitor center open Mon through Sat 10 a.m. to 5 p.m., Sun noon to 5 p.m.; free

Sailor's Creek first appeared on a British-drawn map in the 18th century, but later on the name took on a variety of spellings, including "Sayler's Creek." This Civil War battlefield is part of the "Lee's Retreat" route, which travels from Richmond and Petersburg, across Central Virginia, to its final stopping place at Appomattox—Lee was in retreat, Gen. Philip Sheridan was in pursuit. The Union Army gained the upper hand by attacking the columns of starving Confederate troops as they attempted to head west to Farmville, where supply trains from Lynchburg had rations for 80,000 men. While Lee and some Confederate troops were able to move forward, others behind became engaged with the Union Army in three separate skirmishes, one of which was specifically around Hillsman House, a small wooden clapboard structure that still stands today. Hand-to-hand combat and Union artillery caused heavy losses for the Army of Northern Virginia, with more than 7,400 dead, wounded, or captured, which was one-fourth of Confederate troops in total.

Unlike some of the larger Civil War battlefields, Sailor's Creek is smaller scaled with just one historic structure—Hillsman House—with which to take in an immense story that pitted American against American. Although not open for visitors, interpretation at the visitor center and around the Hillsman House explains in vivid terms how bloody awful the war was, just 72 hours before the bitter end. The Union Army used the house as a field hospital, where amputations were common and bloodstains remain on the floorboards. Amputated limbs were thrown out the front door, collected, and disposed of. The small house was built circa 1780 to 1810 by Moses Overton. His descendant, James Moses Hillsman, lived in the house with his family, although during the year of the Sailor's Creek Battle, Hillsman was a prisoner of war and not at home. His wife, mother, children, and enslaved house laborers were forced to stay in the basement during the battle and listen to the cries of the dying and wounded above.

Members of the family lived in the area right through the 1930s, when the site became part of the state government overseen by nearby Twin Lakes State Park. Sailor's Creek was given National Historic Landmark status in 1985, and in 2008 the historic site became a separate unit of the Virginia State Park system. After viewing the excellent exhibits in the visitor center, head outside and walk the series of trails located in three areas, one of which passes alongside Sailor's Creek and another that starts behind the Hillsman House. All trails are less than a mile long and traverse the low hills, rocky outcroppings, and meadows of Southside Virginia. If you tune out the cars driving through on Saylers Creek Road, there is sun and silence.

Scotchtown
16120 Chiswell Ln., Beaverdam; (804) 227-3500; preservation virginia.org/historic-sites/patrick-henrys-scotchtown; open Mar through Dec, Fri and Sat 10 a.m. to 5 p.m., Sun noon to 5 p.m.; admission charged

If Thomas Jefferson was the pen of the American Revolution, and George Washington the sword, surely Patrick Henry is remembered as the voice. Riding from this house in 1775 to St. John's Episcopal Church in Richmond to give his "Liberty or Death" speech, did Henry know that his words would become indelible in the American mind? His was a voice heard around the world, much like Lexington and Concord was the shot heard around the world.

Scotchtown was Patrick Henry's home and plantation estate from 1771 to 1778—coinciding with the lead up to, and engagement in, the War for Independence. But he left Scotchtown to become the first governor of Virginia, eventually resettling in Charlotte County in Virginia upon his retirement, building a house

there called Red Hill. Scotchtown was built by planter Colonel Charles Chiswell in the 1720s. It is of an elongated shape—93 feet long by 35 feet wide—a seemingly extra-long center hall–shaped structure with an attic floor above (it's easy to imagine children running the full length of the undivided attic). The house was later enlarged and used as a store for selling local tobacco. When Patrick Henry and wife Sarah moved here in 1771, they undoubtedly had high hopes for a full and engaging life. Henry was a young lawyer and political worker, and Sarah had five children to care for. But an easy life was not to be: Sarah became mentally ill after giving birth to their sixth child, was confined to the basement of the house, and eventually died here in 1775. It was not the first sad event in the history of Scotchtown. Earlier, during the ownership of Chiswell, his family was intimately involved with a financial scandal, he brawled with a man and killed him, and he himself is buried somewhere on the grounds in an unmarked grave.

For Henry, though, Scotchtown was not haunted, since he married a second time here in 1777 and then relocated to Williamsburg in 1778 to live in the Governor's Palace. Surely that was a step up for this rural lawyer, who ended up living in the fancy and formal palace surrounded by the elite of Williamsburg (a town he knew well, since he studied at the College of William & Mary at the same time as Thomas Jefferson and was a member of the House of Burgesses in 1763). Scotchtown was acquired by Preservation Virginia in 1958, restored, and given National Historic Landmark designation in 1965, no doubt in preparation for the American bicentennial. On-site you can take a 45-minute tour or a special "Patrick Henry: Champion of Religious Freedom" tour on Sunday at 2 p.m. There is also the option of visiting a self-guided two-room exhibit or tour the grounds with your cell phone for free.

Shack Mountain
1790 Lamb Rd., Charlottesville; private property

Shack Mountain, Monticello, the Rotunda, and the University of Virginia Historic District (or Academical Village in Jeffersonian-speak) are the only National Historic Landmarks in Charlottesville and Albemarle County—and all revolve around Thomas Jefferson. Shack Mountain is the home designed by Fiske Kimball in a near-perfect replication of Thomas Jefferson's Monticello. Kimball (1888–1955) was a scholar of Thomas Jefferson and the history of American architecture and the first chair of the University of Virginia's School of Arts, which included the School of Architecture, which opened in 1919. But, in addition to studying, researching, and writing on the history of architecture, as is often the case, architectural historians are also architects. In Kimball's case, he designed his own home—just as Thomas Jefferson designed his own homes (Monticello and Poplar Forest)—for himself and his wife, Marie Kimball, the first curator of Monticello who also wrote a three-volume biography of the third president.

Often in Virginia large houses and mansions are named for the land on which they were built. So, Monticello is a famous house, but known by that name because

the land on which it was built was already called Monticello. The same holds true for Poplar Forest—the name of the landscape and working plantation on which Jefferson built his retreat home, now identified with that name. Kimball followed this practice by building his home on a small mountain named for the Shackelford family, the derivative of which became the name of his house. Completed in 1937, Shack Mountain is built in a T-form of brick laid in the Flemish bond style (see many other early Virginian buildings of Flemish bond, such as Bacon's Castle). Shack Mountain overlooks Ivy Creek and the Rivanna River. Sir Kenneth Clark, who those old enough will remember as the host of the 1960s television program *Civilsation* and author of the book by the same name, called Shack Mountain a "temple in the woods."

Like Jefferson, who designed and built Poplar Forest as his retirement home, Kimball followed suit with Shack Mountain, although his vision never came to fruition, as his wife Marie died and Kimball followed soon after. This is one of the few National Historic Landmark sites within this book that is privately owned, and therefore not open to visitors. But it is an unusual and late addition to the National Historic Landmark list in Virginia—added in 1992. Kimball's impact on preservation and academic programs in the US was profound. After leaving the University of Virginia, he went on to lead the Philadelphia Museum of Art, to found the Institute of Fine Arts at New York University, and to work on the preservation of iconic Virginia buildings, including Monticello, Gunston Hall, Stratford Hall, and Colonial Williamsburg—each National Historic Landmarks in and of themselves (see separate entries for each).

St. John's Episcopal Church (Historic St. John's Church and Visitor Center)

2401 E. Broad St., Richmond; (804) 648-5015; historicstjohns church.org; open Mon through Sat 10 a.m. 4 p.m., Sun 1 p.m. to 4 p.m. (closed Jan); admission charged

St. John's is an active Episcopal church, but it's not just any historic church sitting high on a hill. Here on March 23, 1775, Patrick Henry, everyone's favorite fiery and sometimes inflammatory American Revolutionary, preached words that echo through the ages: "Give Me Liberty, or Give Me Death!" The events that led up to the beginning of the war—the Boston Tea Party in Boston Harbor, the Battles of Lexington and Concord in Massachusetts, and Patrick Henry's speech to the Second Virginia Convention in Richmond—shaped not only the views of their contemporaries, but the way Americans and others around the world painted a picture of the American Revolution afterward.

St. John's Episcopal Church has a long pre-Revolutionary history, dating to the establishment of several parishes in Virginia during the 17th century. Moving to Richmond in 1741, St. John's needed a new church building and Colonel Richard Randolph, a great-uncle to Thomas Jefferson, built the church from materials donated by William Byrd II, the founder of Richmond. This core of the church remains today as the transept (which is the arm of the church that crosses a nave, or central space). Although this is a common church design, and many such churches were built according to this traditional plan, only four remain in existence today in Virginia. But, St. John's—originally called the Richmond Hill Church among other names—is known more for its role in the Revolution, rather than its architectural heritage. The church was the largest building in Richmond in the 1770s, and thus became a second home to the Second Virginia Convention, an assembly of men that included George Washington, Thomas Jefferson, Richard Henry Lee, and Patrick Henry, who were forced out of Williamsburg, then the capital of the state.

Take the time to visit both inside and outside St. John's. Inside, you can see Patrick Henry's family pew, and if you visit at the right time of the year, St. John's hosts "Liberty or Death" reenactments (check the website for dates) with Patrick Henry himself. More than two centuries later, the fame Henry's oratory brought to the church brings approximately 40,000 visitors annually to St. John's, which became a National Historic Landmark in 1961. After you spend some time walking the churchyard (note the gravesite for George Wythe, whose house is a National Historic Landmark, and described in this book), head into the neighborhood surrounding St. John's—it is one of the oldest neighborhoods in the city (118 acres)

"GIVE ME LIBERTY, OR GIVE ME DEATH !"
PATRICK HENRY delivering his great speech on the Rights of the Colonies, before the Virginia Assembly, convened at Richmond March 23d 1775. Concluding with the above sentiment, which became the war cry of the Revolution.

and contains the most diverse collection of historic buildings in the city, including Federal, Queen Anne, and other 19th-century styles. For this, the area was recognized as a National Historic Landmark District. You can find more history about Patrick Henry by visiting either (or both) of his houses: Scotchtown and Red Hill. Scotchtown is a National Historic Landmark (see separate entry).

Thomas Jefferson's Monticello

931 Thomas Jefferson Pkwy., Charlottesville; (434) 984-9800; home.monticello.org; open year-round except major holidays; many special events; admission charged

Within the realm of Thomas Jefferson and National Historic Landmarks, Monticello gets to be first on the list, because the house, landscape, and people were first in his heart and because without Monticello there would be no University of Virginia Historic District, no Rotunda, and certainly no Shack Mountain.

It's hard to imagine any of the Founding Fathers or Mothers as young adults. Deeply buried in time, wearing powdered wigs and handmade clothes, these first Americans sometimes seem less real people and more mythologized icons who dance around on stage belting out numbers (thanks to productions such as *1776* and *Hamilton*). But even Thomas Jefferson was a young man at one time—and in the year 1757, when the future signer was but 14, his father died. This left Jefferson with the opportunity to pick the choicest of lands his father owned. After choosing Monticello and Montalto, Jefferson finished his schooling, first at William & Mary and then his law studies with George Wythe in Williamsburg and went home to begin building his first house, called Monticello (meaning "little mountain" in Italian). His friends and acquaintances across Virginia lived in wood-frame Colonial homes or large brick mansions designed to look like estates in England. This Virginian chose differently. And in that choice, Jefferson influenced the architectural and cultural style of the US for centuries to come.

The Monticello you visit today is considered the third version—each earlier version was deemed unacceptable to Jefferson's evolving tastes and needs, and he felt no hesitation in pulling down walls and rebuilding. For his mountaintop home, Jefferson turned to a style of architecture called Neoclassical, and he looked backward to the ancient world—Greece and Rome, and then to the Italian Renaissance and the Baroque—to influence his house design. Built of brick shaped by the hands of the enslaved African-American community (for he inherited not just land from his father, but people), the house was based on Andrea Palladio's villas in Northern Italy, with touches of Virginia. Skylights brought in plenty of sunshine when desired, but painted green shutters kept out the strong sun when needed. The house has an octagonal shape, but it is elongated, and its many walls are cut by windows, circulating cooling mountain air. Each room—the entry hallway, Martha's room, the dining room, the parlor, the library, the study, and the bedroom—is a peek into the concerns, joys, and work of the third president, whose open-door policy at Monticello forced him into a retreat to another of his plantations 90 miles south (Poplar Forest, also a National Historic Landmark and described in this book).

Monticello is for everyone: gardeners and gadget lovers, students of African-American history and women's history, and art and architecture buffs. You can park your car, purchase a ticket, and take a van up the mountaintop, or hike the mountain from Kemper Park and travel past Thomas Jefferson and the Jefferson family's gravesite. Once there, the intimate relationship among the president, his family, and the enslaved community who labored and lived on Mulberry Row will become quite apparent. Without them, Thomas Jefferson could not have accomplished the things he did.

Tredegar Iron Works
470 Tredegar St., Richmond National Battlefield Park, Richmond; (804) 819-1934; nps.gov/articles/tredegar-iron-works-ironmaker -to-the-confederacy.htm; open daily 9 a.m. to 5 p.m.; free, but charge for exhibits in partnership with the American Civil War Museum

Along this stretch of the James River are the remains of the Confederacy's most important iron-making facility in the South. Tredegar Iron Works was already well-known when the Civil War broke out in 1861. Named for an ironworks in Tredegar, Wales (UK), Tredegar began in 1836 as a small forge and rolling mill. The site

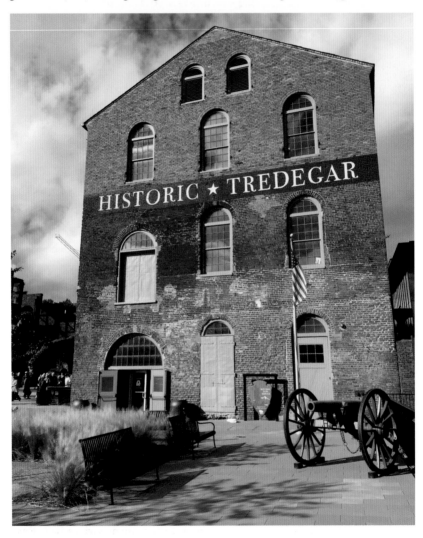

was shared with other milling operations that harnessed water power from the James River and Kanawha Canal (located across the river). In the two decades before the Civil War, Tredegar, along with other smaller foundries, made Richmond the center of iron manufacture. By 1860, under the supervision of Joseph Reid Anderson, Tredegar used about 800 laborers, black and white, free and enslaved. During the Civil War, Tredegar covered nearly five acres and operated day and night to meet the demands of the Confederacy for artillery, ammunition, and other war-related materials. In addition, 1,100 field cannons were made here as the casemates of several Southern warships, including the CSS *Virginia* (which was rebuilt from the scuttled USS *Merrimack* and famously fought the USS *Monitor* at the Battle of Hampton Roads).

Tredegar Iron Works—located in a restored 19th-century brick building with distinctive painting across the facade—contains exhibits and a museum shop, but the place also serves as the visitor center for the whole Richmond National Battlefield Park. From here you can pick up a National Park Service map that outlines Richmond Civil War historic sites that include Chickahominy Bluff Battlefield, Beaver Dam Creek Battlefield, Gaines' Mill Battlefield, Glendale Battlefield, Malvern Hill Battlefield, Cold Harbor Battlefield, Fort Harrison Battlefield, Parker's Battery, Totopotomoy Creek Battlefield, and the Chimborazo Medical Museum. The National Park Service side of operations has free admission, but half of the historic site is managed by a separate, private, not-for-profit entity, the American Civil War Museum. This museum runs the White House and Museum of the Confederacy and the American Civil War Museum in Appomattox.

Tuckahoe Plantation
12601 River Rd., Richmond; (804) 774-1614; tuckahoeplantation .com; house tours by appointment, self-guided landscape tours available except when closed for private events; free

In Virginia, a state seemingly littered with plantation landscapes from north to south and east to west, Tuckahoe Plantation has a special profile: It was the boyhood home of Thomas Jefferson and therefore helps paint a picture of what 18th-century Virginian society was like and how what he experienced here directly shaped his character, and it highlights the network of family relationships over the Commonwealth.

The cultural landscape of Tuckahoe—its buildings, gardens, and landscape—are protected by a preservation easement donated by the current owners, who operate the plantation as a special-event venue (weddings are popular here). While there is a contemporary trend to turn plantation houses and landscapes into wedding venues, the owners of Tuckahoe manage to balance this function with the history of the house and landscape. Historic spaces remain intact and lightly restored, which is very different from the total renovation of other plantations such as Bella Rose

in Lynchburg, which feels more like a commercial enterprise than a sensitive reuse of a historic house and landscape. This is important to consider for any plantation landscape, but especially for one associated with a Founding Father who would also become a slave owner as an adult. Plantations existed because Americans were able to exploit backbreaking labor for free, providing essential value and allowing Virginians, for example, to build generational wealth.

Thomas Jefferson came here as a two-year-old toddler from his birthplace, Shadwell, farther west in Albemarle County. The patriarch was Peter Jefferson, who moved his entire family to Tuckahoe because his wife's cousins, William and Maria Randolph, had died, leaving their three children orphans. William had asked that Peter do this in his will, and the Jeffersons complied, living at Tuckahoe, a circa 1773 house, with their children and the Randolph children for seven years. All of the young ones went to school here, as Peter had a schoolhouse built on-site, as requested by the Randolphs. The one-room squared schoolhouse can still be seen today. The teaching that happened here worked for Thomas—he went on to boarding school, then the College of William & Mary, and finally studied law under the famous George Wythe of Williamsburg, passing the bar exam.

The whole plantation landscape was eventually divided, and today the Lower Tuckahoe landscape is a residential subdivision. Upper Tuckahoe remains intact around the original H-shaped house and its outbuildings. The interior of the house has wood paneling and an ornate wood-carved stairwell. Visitors can tour a series of rooms on the first floor, including the white parlor, saloon, and dining room—food and drink are always of interest to people across time and place. The rooms are richly decorated with a mix of heirlooms, antiques, and chairs that you can sit on, indicating status as a working house in which guests can sit and relax. This is a welcome opportunity from the usual historic house tour, where touching is forbidden!

University of Virginia Historic District (the Academical Village)
Charlottesville; virginia.edu/visit; free access to the grounds, tours available

The fact that Monticello and the University of Virginia (UVA) are the only American house and university on the UNESCO List of World Heritage Sites indicates the global influence of Jefferson's life and work and of the uniqueness of both places. As a lifelong student of the Enlightenment, Thomas Jefferson believed in formal

and informal education, in the separation of church and state, and in the uses of architecture to teach and enlighten the minds of Americans. All of these values came together for Jefferson in the last project of his life: the creation of the first secular college in the US. Although he dreamed it up many years earlier, it wasn't until the last decade of his life that Jefferson had the time—and was able to convince the Virginia State Legislature to devote funds to the project.

The first UVA students arrived on the small campus in 1825. Before their arrival Jefferson had designed the architectural form for the school, selected the professors, created a curriculum, and hired paid laborers and required enslaved laborers to level the ground and construct the buildings. The core of the campus, called the "grounds" in UVA-speak, is the Rotunda (listed by itself as a National Historic Landmark; see separate entry) and the pavilions that extend outward as arms from this central building. Behind the pavilions, which house both professors and students, are gardens growing within Virginia's

"serpentine" walls of red brick. Fourth-year highly accomplished students are given these coveted "lawn rooms," which are literally small rooms with fireplaces that face the lawn—students are still given a cord of wood during the winter and allowed to have fires in their rooms!

UVA was designed by Jefferson in the Neoclassical style (of course—he did not work with any other architectural style and likened the Neoclassical to be the right fit for the US due to its associations with the first democracies in the ancient world), but he presented a twist here: Each pavilion is designed in a different Neoclassical "order" from the Tuscan to the Doric to the Ionic to the Corinthian, so that students would be exposed to and learn from the material world firsthand. Here is an insider's tip on distinguishing the orders of architecture: Look to the capitals—those things sitting on the top of the columns—to see how each one is different as you walk on the lawn, from pavilion to pavilion. People have been building architecture with these forms for more than 2,500 years.

The university has since grown out all around the original "Academical Village," creeping into the surrounding neighborhoods (or is it the neighborhoods came because of the university?). University museums, libraries, public art, and events make UVA an excellent spot for day visits, and there are plenty of restaurants close by, as well as in downtown Charlottesville. During the school year street parking is difficult, so choose one of two parking garages if driving in; otherwise take a bus from downtown Charlottesville—or an Uber!

Rotunda, University of Virginia

University of Virginia, Charlottesville; (434) 924-7969; rotunda
.virginia.edu; open daily 9 a.m. to 5 p.m.; free tours offered during
the academic year

The Rotunda sits at the heart of the University of Virginia's Academical Village, and it is easy to see why. Designed by Thomas Jefferson as a temple to education, the retired president looked to the ancient world yet again for inspiration. He found the circular plan of the Pantheon in Rome to be the right model for this building, although instead of placing statues to the gods in niches within the space, Jefferson intended the Rotunda to house the university library. Built of brick with Neoclassical details such as porches with columns and pediments, the Rotunda has a dome with a skylight, just as the Pantheon does, with an oculus or "eye" opening up to the skies above.

The Rotunda, like many buildings in history, burned at the end of the 19th century. The well-known American architect of the Gilded Age, Stanford White was brought in to renovate the interior—a good fit considering that adherents to the Beaux Arts tradition in architecture, as White was, relied on classical forms, just as Jefferson had done generations earlier. But this rebuild was not to last. In 1976, the year of America's bicentennial celebrations, the interior was gutted again and rebuilt according to Jefferson's original plans.

The wings or arms of student rooms extend out from the Rotunda and contain the pavilions mentioned in the UVA Historic District entry, which housed the

professors. The builders began their work in 1822 and finished in 1826, the year after the school opened for studies, making it the last building completed on campus and also the finale to Jefferson's life: He died on July 4 of that year, and the Rotunda was finished a few months afterward. We know that Jefferson thought the creation of the University of Virginia an important milestone in the development of the country—on his gravestone (which you can view at Monticello) he had the following carved: "Here was buried Thomas Jefferson, Author of the Declaration of

American Independence, Of the Statute of Virginia for religious freedom & Father of the University of Virginia." If you step outside to the street facade of the Rotunda, you will see a Gilded Age bronze statue of Jefferson, high on a plinth. The figure holds a document representing the Statute of Religious Freedom, which passed the Virginia General Assembly in 1786. Sadly this statue was also the focus on the Unite the Right rally in August 2017—one of the many twists and turns around the figure of Thomas Jefferson in the 21st century.

It's a wonder to think that new things can be discovered about such famous buildings, but that is just what happened in 2016, when, during a renovation of the Rotunda's basement, a chemical hearth for a laboratory was discovered, which can now be viewed. The public is welcome to visit the Rotunda and use its spaces for reading and contemplation—just as Thomas Jefferson intended.

Virginia State Capitol
1000 Bank St. (access via the Capitol Visitor's Center), Richmond; (804) 698-1788; virginiacapitol.gov; open Mon through Sat 9 a.m. to 5 p.m., Sun 1 p.m. to 5 p.m.; guided tours available; free

The Commonwealth of Virginia remembers 1619 as the year the first legislative body was established by English colonists in North America (at Williamsburg) and also the year the first enslaved people of color were brought, again, to the English Colonies. The Virginia State Capitol demonstrates Virginia's long shadow on the history of the US. Built in 1788 from plans drawn up by Thomas Jefferson and French architect Charles-Louis Clèrisseau, the State Capitol building is the third oldest in the country.

Due to Jefferson's influence, Richmond became the state capital of Virginia in 1780. Not only did Jefferson move the capital from Williamsburg to Richmond, he also designed the building that is still used today. From France, where he was ambassador, Jefferson drafted letters and drawings for the new capitol, and he even had a plaster model made that was shipped to Richmond, which you can see inside the building. The foundation stone was laid for this building on August 18, 1785— during the tenure of Patrick Henry as the first state governor of Virginia (Thomas Jefferson would become the second). Although the building was changed considerably when wings of offices were added in the early 20th century, Jefferson's belief in the Classical style of architecture as being the right one for American government is an idea that took hold here and impacted local and state capitals around the country, including the national capital in Washington, D.C. Americans are quite used to seeing columns, pediments, and white marble statuary—not because this is how things were done in Europe, but because this is how Jefferson did it right here in Richmond, Virginia.

When this building first gained status as a National Historic Landmark in 1960, its designated name and content recognition was as the Capitol of the Confederacy or the Confederate Capitol. It was not until 2016 that the Virginia Department of Historic Resources, which also manages the Virginia Historical Highway Marker program, worked to change the designation to better reflect the full history of the building—not just its Confederate past, but also its architectural and decorative arts significance, as a model. Today the building is half working government center and

half history and art museum. (How many state capitols do you know that have a full-service visitor center on-site, complete with coffee shop?). The historic core of the building contains statuary of many of the American presidents who were also Virginians, including the famous full-length marble of George Washington in the Rotunda, done by Jean-Antoine Houdon and commissioned by Thomas Jefferson and Benjamin Franklin. Both men knew something about the importance of image and identity in creating meaning for the public.

Outside the Virginia State Capitol are a number of equally impressive land-marks to see—on your way to the Virginia Governor's Mansion (see separate entry), you will be able to view up close the 21-foot-tall bronze monument to George Washington (and including smaller figures of other Virginians who played roles in the Revolution, including Thomas Jefferson and Patrick Henry). The newest addition to Capitol Square is the State of Virginia's first monument to women, titled *Voices from the Garden: The Virginia Women's Monument*, featuring the figures of four women important to the history of Virginia.

Virginia Governor's Mansion (the Executive Mansion)
Ninth and Grace Sts., Capitol Square, Richmond; executivemansion .virginia.gov; open for tours, check website for details; free

What was once perhaps taken for granted—a handsome, large house for the governor of Virginia, a place to relax perhaps after a day of working in the State Capitol across the square—is currently in the spotlight and under critical scrutiny. All of this is due to Governor Ralph Northam's recent admission that he bears responsibility for a photograph of two men in blackface who appeared in his medical college year-book. This is surely an unusual way to introduce a National Historic Landmark, and it's hard to imagine this happening anywhere else, but in Virginia and in Richmond, perhaps not. The legacies of enslavement, Jim Crow, and racial inequities cast long shadows over the South—but especially here in the urbane capital city, where the shock of seeing such things was thought to be a part of the past.

The current critical moment in local, state, and American history aside, the Virginia Governor's Mansion has had a long history and has seen a lot of action: It is the second-oldest executive mansion—only after the White House—to be in continual, original use. The Virginia Governor's Mansion is a rectangular, two-story brick structure constructed between 1811 and 1813. Designed by Alexander Parris in the Federal style (which is English or Georgian in origin, but changes name after the establishment of the new country), the mansion replaced an earlier wood-frame house that served as the first governor's residence in Richmond, after the capital was moved here from Williamsburg under Thomas Jefferson's direction in 1780. The original mansion design was basically a plantation-type house in the city. There was a cookhouse, smokehouse, stable, icehouse, and carriage house located on the grounds around the main house, just as there would be in the country. It's likely there were kitchen gardens, too. Today only three of these original structures remain (the mansion house, the cookhouse, and the carriage house).

To modernize the mansion, several restorations and additions happened over the course of the 20th century, including one project documented by Bob Vila on his long-running program *Home Again* (if house restoration is your interest, see a

series of videos showcasing the work at bobvila.com). Alexander Parris's design was complemented more than a century later by the addition of formal gardens designed by Charles Gillette, which took the place of the original working landscape. Inside the fence surrounding the Governor's Mansion, you can find the remaining historic structures; step outside the gate but still within Capitol Square, and you can see the Bell Tower, the Patrick Henry Office Building, Old City Hall, and various monuments (mentioned in the Virginia State Capitol entry). This house, throughout all of its changes and updates, has seen a wide range of visiting dignitaries, including Queen Elizabeth II; Presidents Rutherford B. Hayes, Theodore Roosevelt, and Barack Obama; as well as Winston Churchill and Charles Lindbergh. Although there is a current state of crisis in the Virginia Governor's Mansion, if you take the long view of history—of a building that survived a Civil War and more—the business of state government will go on, regardless of who is in power.

White House of the Confederacy (part of the American Civil War Museum)

1201 E. Clay St., American Civil War Museum, Richmond; (804) 649-1861; acwm.org; call for tour schedule; admission charged

There is, of course, no other city in the US that can claim to have a state capitol designed by Thomas Jefferson, in addition to the mansion designated the White House of the Confederacy, where Jefferson Davis lived as president of the Confederate States of America from 1861 to 1865. The first White House of the Confederacy was in Montgomery, Alabama. The Confederate States of America (the Confederacy) then chose to move to Richmond for the city's many features that would be useful in time of war: although not the South's largest city, its location on the James River, a major waterway that traveled across the interior of the state, from the mountains to the Chesapeake Bay; the number of ironworks such as Tredegar (see separate entry); and the number of railroads that emanated out from the city, connecting to the Deep South states. All of these features gave Richmond a distinct advantage. This would prove to be true, as Richmond, though besieged, was not taken until the end of the war, unlike Northern Virginia cities such as Alexandria and Fredericksburg.

Robert Mills designed this mansion, not far from his other Richmond architectural work Monumental Church (see separate entry). Private things happened to the Davis family in this house. Their daughter Winnie, the "First Daughter of the Confederacy" was born here, and their son Joseph died here after falling off a porch. When the Battles of Richmond and Petersburg were fought in the spring of 1865, the end of the Confederacy was near. Jefferson Davis fled this house with his family on April 3, and six days later Lee surrendered to Grant at Appomattox and the Confederate States of America, and Davis's presidency, were no more. The house today is a part of the American Civil War Museum and holds one of the world's largest and most significant collection of Confederate materials in the country.

CHESAPEAKE BAY

Holly Knoll, R. R. Moton Home
6496 Allmondsville Rd., Gloucester; gloucesterinstitute.org; private property

Holly Knoll is the Georgian-style retirement home of Robert Russa Moton (1867–1940), an African-American educator and humanitarian who led the Hampton Institute as well as the Tuskegee Institute in the 20th century. Although Georgian in style, the house was built in the modern age—1935—when Moton retired to the rural countryside of Gloucester County, away from the bustle of Hampton Roads and Virginia Beach. Holly Knoll overlooks the York River, which today makes it a reflective setting for the Gloucester Institute, an organization dedicated to cultivating a think-tank atmosphere for creativity and building solutions of and for minority communities. Leadership, career development, and scholarship are the heart of the Gloucester Institute, building on the legacy left by Moton, whose name appears in this book in Farmville: Schools were named for the educator across Virginia and beyond (see separate entry on p. 30).

The house features the elements of standard issue Georgian-style brick houses of Virginia, including dormer windows, a portico with balustrade, and a gable roof.

Under the roofline there are multiple bedrooms on the second and third floors, making Holly Knoll an appropriate setting for a retreat and conference center. The property also includes a reproduction log home, to demonstrate where Moton and many others like him grew up. Inside the home several pieces of furniture remain from Moton's era, even though the house has a contemporary use. Although the house is of interest, it is the life and work of Moton that provides Holly Knoll its National Historic Landmark status; it is the only house still standing from Moton's life, and therefore it acts as a representation for all of the important work accomplished in African-American education and Civil Rights.

Moton was one of the founders of the National Urban League, a now historic civil rights organization dedicated to economic development addressing urban communities across the US. He then went on to transform the Tuskegee Institute from an agricultural and trade school to a college and professional institution. His work was known in political and activist communities—he eventually became an adviser to five US presidents, from Woodrow Wilson to Franklin Delano Roosevelt. Moton traveled to France during World War I to inspect African-American troops on behalf of the Wilson administration. He published three books over the course of his lifetime and won numerous awards, including honorary degrees from Oberlin and Williams Colleges and Howard, Virginia Union, Wilberforce, Lincoln, and Harvard Universities.

Menokin
4037 Menokin Rd., Warsaw; (804) 333-1776; menokin.org; open 7 a.m. to 7 p.m.; free to walk the property, $15 to visit the historic site, $5 for self-guided tour

Menokin was the home of Francis Lightfoot Lee, a signer of the Declaration of Independence, and his wife Rebecca Tayloe. This is interesting enough in and of itself, but the real reason people pay attention to Menokin today is due to the historic home status of this National Historic Landmark. The interest has to do with the unique and progressive preservation of the circa 1769 house. Because, you see, the house is in ruins, and instead of completely rebuilding, the Menokin Foundation decided on a new way to preserve and interpret the ruins: stabilize the collapsed structure with steel and glass walls, which will allow visitors to experience the architecture and size of the original house, while displaying pieces of the house—such as hand-planed architectural decorations—in a specially built visitor center and interpretation center. The organization calls Menokin a "great preservation adventure," because this type of work is new in the American context and the work is a jigsaw puzzle of pieces to fit back together.

Menokin is one of the best-documented 18th-century houses in Virginia and one of only a very few pre–Revolution era houses whose original drawings still exist (the

drawings were, in fact, found in the attic at Mount Airy, see separate entry). Though the house is partially collapsed, approximately 80 percent of its original materials survive—although much was pulled from the house before collapse or later pulled from piles of collapsed material. Slowly, with the work of architectural historians, conservators, archaeologists, and others, the pieces of the house are identified, conserved, and put on view. For example, the exquisite woodwork from Menokin's interior and excavated structural elements are on display at the Menokin Foundation's King Conservation and Visitors Center on-site. Because of this preservation strategy and the amount of work done over the years in documenting its history (the house was still standing until the 1950s), it is possible to get a sense of what life was like here on the Northern Neck of Virginia, where farms and the tidal rivers encouraged a peaceful setting that remains intact today.

The Menokin Foundation sees their work in a broad context. Not only is the historic site taking the lead to save this house, but doing it in a way that engages visitors with the process and techniques of preservation. Visitors experience the site through touch—something not encouraged in most museums and historic houses—and view the work happening every day. In addition, the foundation sees itself as a catalyst for an economically challenged area, working in collaboration with other Northern Neck entities to create jobs, training, and enrichment programs for their local community, not just to draw in visitors. Finally, the Menokin Foundation manages the 500-acre property, more than half of which is in the Rappahannock River Valley National Wildlife Refuge. So, when you are done touring the visitor center and viewing the house exhibit under glass, take a long walk on the scenic property that surrounds Menokin, or better yet, grab one of the free-to-use kayaks from the landing area and have your own Captain John Smith adventure. Trail maps are available.

Stratford Hall

483 Great House Rd., Stratford; (804) 493-8038; stratfordhall.org; guided and self-guided house tours available year-round, "Grounds Pass" available for the hiking trails, shoreline, gardens, public grounds, and shop; admission charged

Before *Hamilton*, there was the Broadway musical *1776*. One of the many bright and award-winning tunes from *1776* is "The Lees of Old Virginia," in which Richard Henry Lee sings about the FFV or, the First Families of Virginia. No family had as many participants in the founding of Virginia, and the founding of the US, than the Lees—thus, when Richard Henry Lee sings, "You see it's here a Lee! There a Lee! And everywhere a Lee, a Lee!" he isn't exaggerating. Richard and his brother Francis Lightfoot Lee were the only brothers to sign the Declaration of Independence. They were preceded by generations of Lees serving in political offices dating to the early 17th century. Stratford Hall was their ancestral home, a plantation, and then the birthplace of their most famous descendant, Robert Edward Lee (born here in 1807), the Confederacy's general-in-chief. Later, in early the 20th century, Stratford Hall would turn into a shrine of sorts for Robert E. Lee and the Lee family, but by then the days of the Lee political dynasty were long over. (Francis Lightfoot Lee's own home, Menokin, is described in a separate entry.)

The house and its current programming have evolved over the past century and a half, reflecting social changes that incorporate much more into the interpretation of this historic mansion and plantation landscape. One Thomas Lee began the story by erecting this house in the late 1730s—a Georgian H-plan of red brick (of course— it's Virginia!) with eight chimneys, which is unique in its layout among Colonial plantation houses of the Northern Neck. Inside the house are a series of historically furnished rooms, the most notable of which is the Great Hall, a huge 30-foot-square paneled space intended to impress visitors and made for dancing. This is the only

room in the mansion with reproduction furniture, which is helpful for allowing visitors to feel comfortable sitting, or even standing, on the original floors, which are a
glowing Virginia yellow pine. Originally consisting of more than 6,000 acres with
a view and access to the Potomac River, the historic site today maintains a rural,

rambling feeling. Outbuildings, walking paths, shoreline, and multiple landscape features—including the enslaved persons' cemetery and quarters, a reconstructed gristmill, and the Payne Memorial Cabin, a log cabin built as a memorial to Wesley Payne, a descendant still living on on-site when Stratford Hall was purchased by the Robert E. Lee Association in 1929—make visiting Stratford Hall a layered, multi-sensory event. Inside the house a new tour via self-guided audio integrates the voices of different people living, working, and visiting Stratford Hall.

Stratford Hall was made a National Historic Landmark in 1960, but work continues on the preservation of the house and landscape. Visitors come to Stratford Hall for history, but fans of the prehistoric world come to explore the prehistoric cliffs over the Potomac, which regularly expel fossils millions of years old, as well as coveted shark teeth. Unlike most historic house museums, Stratford Hall has an inn on-site as well as a full-service restaurant, making a weekend or two-day visit easy and helping you access the site in remote Westmoreland County. You can stay here and use Stratford Hall as your home base to explore vineyards and wineries, birding trails, more Founding Father houses, or kayak the waterways.

Yeocomico Church
233 Old Yeocomico Rd., Kinsale; (804) 472-2593; copleparish.com/ yeocomico-church, still-functioning church, open for self-guided tours the last Sat during summer months

Although this is the fourth-oldest church in Virginia, the history of Yeocomico has not always been secure. The church, originally part of the Anglican Church, was abandoned by the early 19th century. Today it operates as one of the churches in the Cople Episcopal Parish of Westmoreland County, but visitors are welcome. Yeocomico—a name Native American in origin, which is also the name of the nearby river—is a unique architectural expression of early historic Virginia: a brick building that brings together European elements from the Gothic and the Georgian, together with the vernacular, or local, tradition. There is nothing else like it in Virginia, and perhaps anywhere else.

The parish was formed in 1662 here in the Northern Neck, on a peninsula of red Virginia soil surrounded by the waters of the Chesapeake Bay. Many of the colonies' earliest churches were built of wood framing, and thus most of the first-generation Christian churches on North American soil do not survive. The second building on-site, of variegated brick, provided Yeocomico with a longer life span, although there were challenges to its preservation after the American Revolution. Local tradition states that Revolutionary soldiers used the church as a barracks, although things get worse from here. These soldiers were also said to have slaughtered animals in the church, right on the communion table, leaving bloodstains. Later the church was

left vacant, making it attractive to vandals and a second story about soldierly abuse: A patrol of American soldiers during the War of 1812 used the baptismal font as a drinking bowl, which was later found in a nearby farm field. During the Civil War, Confederate soldiers bunked here. These kinds of stories give color to a building that warrants such storytelling. Architectural historians have difficulty in pinpointing the style of the church that is a mixture of sophistication and the archaic. In the end, most describe Yeocomico Church as charming.

The Northern Neck is a remote place even today, so the architecture of this church may derive both from the English traditions of the settlers and their culture, but also from the whims of the builders who did not attend schools or have great exposure to architectural history. The builder and craftsmen are unknown, but they would have likely designed Yeocomico Church using architectural pattern books and perhaps the conversation of the local church fathers. Due to its remote location and disuse, Yeocomico didn't get electricity until 1947 and a heating system until 1949. There are many architectural details to enjoy here; most important is the medieval-style wicket door (a door within a door—look at the picture), which is thought to be the only one surviving in the US. The Jacobean-style table and octagonal baptismal font date from the church's 17th-century origins. A date of 1706 inscribed in the brickwork may indicate the erection of the brick building, which incorporated elements of the earlier timber frame structure.

Old Cape Henry Lighhouse, see entry on p. 73

COASTAL VIRGINIA

Adam Thoroughgood House

1636 Parish Rd., Virginia Beach; (757) 385-5100; museumsvb.org/room/thoroughgood-house; open Thurs through Sat 10 a.m. to 4 p.m.; admission charged

When Virginians think of Virginia Beach, it's usually the beach—not Virginia history—that comes to mind. But there are early historic houses here that have survived 300 years to document those early days, including the Adam Thoroughgood House, a circa 1719 brick structure built on the Lynnhaven River. The Adam Thoroughgood House is one of four properties administered by the City of Virginia Beach History Museums, a municipal department. The other properties—all worth visiting—are the Lynnhaven House, just a few years younger than the Thoroughgood House (circa 1725) and of the same early Virginia Colonial style; the Francis Land House; and the Union Kempsville High School Museum, the first school for African Americans in Princess Anne County (now known as Virginia Beach). An early settler of Princess Anne County, Argall Thorowgood established his family seat here, although he died at age 35 before the house was finished. His wife Susannah finished the construction and lived here with their son John, who would add the

interior decorations for which the house is known, including paneling and wainscotting, both English traditions in domestic architecture.

The first Adam Thoroughgood (his name becoming Americanized over time) arrived in Virginia as an indentured servant in 1622. This process brought many poor people from England to the Colonies, with the intent of working for seven years freely in exchange for the passage. Thoroughgood was fortunate to finish his years of service, became a member of colonial society, and started building wealth for his descendants. Building wealth was primarily done through land acquisition, which provided voting rights, and eventually for Thoroughgood, a place in the House of Burgesses. The house is small, originally two rooms built on two floors in a medieval style with a steeply pitched roofline and chimneys at either end. There are casement windows, which feature small panes of diamond-shaped cut glass—a telltale sign of 17th-century architecture in the colonies—and a combination of English- and Flemish-style brickwork.

As far as historic house museums go in Virginia, the Adam Thoroughgood House is a late arrival, having been purchased, restored, and opened to the public in 1957, and has since undergone thorough restoration and preservation work. The City of Virginia Beach History Museums runs multiple programs out of its newly built Thoroughgood Education Center. Outside the house are formal English-style gardens. Today there is only four-fifths of an acre left of the original 5,000. This is another of many properties that became a National Historic Landmark in Virginia in 1960. While the house is architecturally significant due to its early age and location, Adam Thoroughgood is partly the reason for the house's landmark status: He came from King's Lynn in Norfolk, England, and many geographic place-names in Virginia Beach are tied to him, including the Lynnhaven River and the City of Norfolk.

Bacon's Castle
465 Bacon's Trl., Surry; (757) 357-5976; preservationvirginia.org/historic-sites/bacons-castle; weekend hours Mar through Dec; admission charged

The oldest brick dwelling in North America—that's an attention grabber, surely! But there is more. Bacon's Castle, built in the 1660s, was the scene of the first rebellion against the English Crown on American soil (the slightest glimmer of things to come—taxes were involved). Driving out to the historic site in Surry County is like traveling through time. The low-lying landscape remains mostly intact, agricultural, and isolated. The Jacobean-style architecture of the house is the last remaining sample in the US, and only two other examples exist in the Western Hemisphere—both in Barbados. Although built in the Colony of Virginia, this house might lead visitors to think about the British Atlantic World—a world of trade and travel.

Bacon's Castle is named for Nathanial Bacon, the man who led the rebellion, although he is not known to have actually visited the house. The owner of the house was Arthur Allen, an immigrant who arrived from England in 1649, and thus the structure was called "Allen's Brick House." Bacon's followers used the house after burning down Jamestown in 1676 for perceived abuses by the governor, representative of the king. Thousands of men were involved with the attack, and more than 80 of them ended up here, pillaging and destroying property as they fled retaliation. Bacon's men took over the castle, eating everything in sight, slaughtering his animals, and making mayhem. Many were eventually captured and hung or fined, but the story of Bacon's Rebellion became part of history, and eventually Allen's Brick House became known as Bacon's Castle.

The Jacobean architectural features on the house denote its European style: There are triple-stacked chimneys, shaped Flemish gables, and carved compass roses decorating the crossbeams in many rooms. The style of brickwork is called Flemish bond, which creates a patterned surface and would become a model for architectural design for Virginia across the 18th century and later. The house was surrounded by a formal garden in the English style, some of which has been laid out again after excavations. The state of Virginia is a center for horticultural enterprises, both private and commercial. Virginians love their formal gardens. The garden at Bacon's Castle is considered the earliest English garden in North America. Until very recently boxwoods reigned supreme in Virginia gardens. Unfortunately, boxwood blight is taking many of them, some that had been growing for more than 150 years near historic houses.

Designated a National Historic Landmark in 1960, Bacon's Castle doesn't exist unchanged. For example, during the 19th century an original one-story service wing was replaced by a taller, boxier two-story wing, and the original diamond-pane casement windows (with smaller slivers of glass) were replaced by double-hung sash windows. Preservation Virginia, the manager of the house and landscape, recently celebrated the 350th anniversary of Bacon's Castle—a landmark birthday for a landmark house.

Berkeley Plantation

12602 Harrison Landing Rd., Charles City; (804) 829-6018; berkeleyplantation.com; open daily year-round 9:30 a.m. to 4:30 p.m.; admission charged

There are Virginia plantations, and then there is Berkeley. Who else has the stature to challenge Plymouth Plantation in Massachusetts in calling itself the place of the first Thanksgiving in the New World? Berkeley Plantation does—and it has a Virginia Historical Highway Marker sign to prove it! The James River Plantations of Charles City County astound with their number, age, and history. They are evocative because they are so old, and in some ways feel unchanged. The James River still floats by, as it always has, and the trees and grasses still turn to green every spring. But in the 21st century, these plantation houses are under new scrutiny—old-timey representations of "gracious living" as an interpretive theme for tourism has had its day. People today want to know: What was life really like for all of the people who lived here, including those hundreds of individuals and families enslaved? How did the events that happened here affect the history of the country? Inquiring minds ask these kinds of questions and visit historic plantations such as Berkeley to tease out answers to complicated issues.

Berkeley Plantation has permanent residents. The Jamieson family, who have lived at Berkeley since the early 20th century and worked to ensure its preservation, continue to live on the upper two floors. The first owners of Berkeley, the Harrisons, like many Southern families who came to the end of the Civil War, did not have the

means to keep the plantation working. The Southern economy was in ruins, and the free labor enjoyed for so long was forever abolished. But it was a Scottish immigrant from New York who heard of the sale by auction of Berkeley, came to the rescue of the house and one thousand acres of land, and preserved it for use, study, and enjoyment.

John Jamieson knew Berkeley Plantation's reputation. The house and landscape had had famous owners. The second Benjamin Harrison was a signer of the Declaration of Independence and three times governor of Virginia. His son, William Henry Harrison, called on the campaign trail "Tippecanoe," was the ninth president of the US. His grandson, Benjamin Harrison, in turn, became the 23rd president of the US. Surely the Harrisons rival the Lees in the impact one family has made on the nation's political history. But Thomas Jefferson (never far when studying Virginia history), was here, too, providing the suggestion that two of the interior first-floor spaces be opened by using archways and connecting woodwork. And then there's Jefferson's enemy, Benedict Arnold, who makes an appearance at Berkeley along the James in 1781, burning and ransacking his way to Richmond and back. Most of the furniture in the house was pulled outside and destroyed, which foreshadowed Berkeley's fate during the Civil War: The house and plantation were occupied by McClellen's Army of the Potomac from 1861 to 1865, and by the end of the war, the contents were gone again. But, John Jamieson, a drummer boy for the Union Army, remembered Berkeley—everyone remembers Berkeley—and became the Northern rescuer of this most Southern house.

Bruton Parish Church
331 W. Duke of Gloucester St., Williamsburg; (757) 229-2891; brutonparish.org; open to visitors outside of service hours; free

Bruton Parish was consolidated out of two earlier churches in 1674. Like many Virginia personal and place-names, Bruton traces its name to England—Bruton was the ancestral home of Sir William Berkeley, whose descendant house in the American Colonies, Berkeley Plantation, is a National Historic Landmark, also described in this book. The original church on-site was deemed too small, and perhaps too

Gothic, and plans were made in the early 1700s to erect the colony's first cruciform church in a Neoclassical style. Bruton was finished in 1715 and became the parish for the Williamsburg political elite, centered close to the Governor's Palace and Capitol of Virginia, which had moved from Jamestown. By the time of George Washington, Thomas Jefferson, and Patrick Henry—who all worshipped here—Bruton was more than a religious home; the parish was part of political life, as when Boston Harbor was blocked by the British in retaliation for the Boston Tea Party. Burgesses (elected white men serving in the legislature of the colony) marched through

Williamsburg in protest and ended their march at Bruton Parish Church with a Day of Fasting, Humiliation, and Prayer. George Wythe, whose house is a National Historic Landmark (see separate entry), was a vestry member here—a member of the House of Burgesses, considered a revolutionary radical.

Of course it was not long before Bruton, like all of Williamsburg, became embroiled in the American Revolution. The war and the creation of a new country had an ill effect on Bruton: the capitol of the Colony of Virginia, now the Commonwealth of Virginia, was moved to Richmond and the Anglican Church (i.e., the Church of England) in Virginia was dissolved. Bruton's finances dwindled and the 19th century brought even more hardship—an early restoration of the church decimated its interior decorations and furniture, and soon the Civil War came knocking on the front door. After the war, Virginia entered a period of rebuilding, and Bruton Parish Church was stabilized once again, although it would take the vision of its 29th rector, the Rev. Dr. W.A.R. Goodwin, to understand the historical value of the architecture of the church and find the financial support to fund the work needed to bring Bruton back to its original colonial form.

Bruton Parish Church was just one colonial-era building of many that needed attention in Williamsburg. In 1907 Bruton had been restored—just in time for tercentennial of the founding of the Episcopal Church in Virginia—but Goodwin became a rector/restorer when he realized that, in fact, much of Williamsburg's colonial-era buildings were not getting the professional attention that Bruton Parish Church received and that these buildings would be lost if something didn't happen quickly. With some work Goodwin attracted the philanthropic attention of John D. Rockefeller Jr., and his wife Abby Aldrich Rockefeller, the heirs to Standard Oil. Although Rockefeller's name is associated with the creation of Colonial Williamsburg today, Goodwin played an intrinsic role in the shaping of one of the most successful living museums in US history. Colonial Williamsburg opened its doors—a lot of doors actually!—to the public in the 1930s. In total more than 500 buildings were restored or re-created, buildings from the 19th century and later were demolished, and a massive tourism enterprise grew up from the first project at Bruton.

Cape Henry Lighthouse
583 Atlantic Ave., Fort Story; preservationvirginia.org/historic-sites/ cape-henry-lighthouse; open daily year-round (check website); tours stop 30 minutes prior to closing; admission charged

The only National Historic Landmark on this historic spit of land (the Delmarva Peninsula was settled in 1634 as one Virginia's original eight counties), the Cape Henry Lighthouse is not Virginia's only lighthouse—there are many others, including a few from the 19th century—but it is the oldest commissioned lighthouse

structure in the US. Built in 1792, Cape Henry Lighthouse was commissioned by President George Washington, who authorized the building of the lighthouse under the new document governing the country: the Constitution (adopted in 1787). A sum of $15,200 was granted for the construction, which was overseen by Alexander Hamilton, then secretary of the treasury. As if this weren't enough of a draw for lighthouse aficionados, there is more: a second lighthouse, built in 1881, which is painted black and white. Together, both lighthouses are part of the National Historic Landmark listing. A double lighthouse on the southern tip of the peninsula is not unusual, when considering the amount of water traffic traveling close by since the 17th century. Chesapeake Bay and the Atlantic coastline are an underwater graveyard for ships not successful in navigating these waters.

Considered the first public works project of the American federal government, the earliest lighthouse, or the "Old" Cape Henry Light, was built in Aquia sandstone, which is the same material used to build much of Washington, D.C. At the base of the lighthouse is a small memorial center that functions as the visitor center to purchase tickets to climb the lighthouse and to get souvenirs. Although the lighthouse keeper's house is not open to the public, many early lighthouse keepers wrote of their experiences doing this important work, including Willis Augustus Hodges, Cape Henry's first African-American lighthouse keeper. Hodges, like all lighthouse keepers, would have to clean the tower daily, inspect and polish the lens, and clean the glass in the lantern room to ensure visibility. Today visitors take photos from the lantern room of the beauty of the Chesapeake Bay and coastline. For hundreds of years this beauty was seen through the lens of the dangers of the age of sail and steam.

Managed today by Preservation Virginia, the lighthouse is not an easy place to find and access: Cape Henry Lighthouse is on US military grounds, the Joint Expeditionary Base Fort Story to be exact, and all visitors must stop at the entrance gate to the military base. In late 2018 a new shuttle service was implemented at Gate 8 to help visitors access the lighthouses more easily (before, visitors would have to stop at the gate, have their car searched, and fill out a form). A valid ID is required for everyone over the age of 16 to enter, and a driver must have both car registration and

proof of insurance. Although it takes some work, it is interesting to drive through Fort Story to the lighthouses, which are located close to the "First Landing" site where English settlers visited before making their way to Jamestown for settlement. The second lighthouse, the black-and-white striped New Cape Henry Light, is not open for visitors, but is historic in its own right and photogenic. Close by is the Cape Henry Memorial, managed by the National Park Service.

Fort Monroe National Monument
41 Bernard Rd., Fort Monroe; (757) 722-3678; nps.gov/fomr/index .htm; open year-round; free admission to the Casemate Museum and to walk the grounds

Fort Monroe is one of the newest National Park Service units in the country, becoming a National Monument in 2011. There are few other American fort sites with so much history to preserve and interpret—a long visit is needed to walk the peninsula, take in the views, visit the museum, examine the architecture, and photograph the birdlife. In 1619 "20 and odd" African people were brought to the Virginia Colony at Point Comfort, the oldest fort on-site, an event around which American Evolution, initiating a series of statewide events, commemorated in 2019 (see americanevolution2019.com), along with other major historical "firsts" for Virginia and North America.

Completed in 1834 and named for President James Monroe, Fort Monroe is the largest stone fort built in the US. The location was vital to the coastal defense of the Chesapeake Bay for hundreds of years. Many stories centered in and around Fort Monroe are told in the Casemate Museum, including those involving well-known figures such as Edgar Allan Poe, who entered the US Army after leaving the University of Virginia due to financial hardships. Poe was at Fort Monroe from 1828 to

1829, and left to enroll at West Point, whereas West Point–trained engineer Robert E. Lee and his wife Mary Custis Lee spent time at the fort in the years 1831 to 1834. During the Civil War, spectators on the ramparts at Fort Monroe watched the Battle of the Ironclad ships USS *Monitor* and CSS *Virginia* (*Merrimack*). Finally at the end of the war, president of the Confederate States of America Jefferson Davis was imprisoned here—visitors can step inside his cell, which houses a simple bed and desk. But the most inspiring story of Fort Monroe during the Civil War was its use as a safe haven for enslaved people who slipped across Confederate lines to the Union-held Fort Monroe. This practice started with three men building Confederate

gun lines who came to Fort Monroe for refuge. The fort's commander Major General Benjamin Butler negated the legality of the Fugitive Slave Act and refused to turn the men in to the Confederates, reasoning that they were considered "contraband" property by the Confederacy and thus could be kept as contraband of war. Soon, word spread that Fort Monroe was a safe place, and "contraband camps" of African Americans sprang up around the fort. This history earned Fort Monroe the nickname "Freedom's Fortress."

Fort Monroe, all 565 acres of it, is a "park-in-progress" managed through a private and public collaborative intent on rehabilitating the area for education and visitor use, with residential and commercial activity. The entities doing this work are the Fort Monroe Authority of the Commonwealth of Virginia, the National Park Service, and the City of Hampton.

George Wythe House
101 Palace Green St., Williamsburg; (888) 965-7254; colonial williamsburg.com/locations/george-wythe-house; open every day except Mon and Wed; Colonial Williamsburg ticket needed to enter

George Wythe's name may not be very well-known outside of Virginia, but to this state and its history, Wythe (1726–1806) is a colossus. This is a man who taught Thomas Jefferson, John Marshall, and generations of others in the study of law; was a signer of the Declaration of Independence and the US Constitution; designed the seal of Virginia, still in place today as seen on the state flag; and was a judge and justice of the peace. Oddly, he is also the only person associated with a National Historic Landmark in Virginia to have been murdered.

The George Wythe House in Williamsburg is the only house standing and open to the public that interprets the life and work of Wythe, even though he did not commission, build, nor design the house himself. When Wythe married Elizabeth Taliaferro, her father gave them the house as a gift, since Wythe spent his working days in Williamsburg at the House of Burgesses, in the company of his friends with whom

he discussed politics and philosophy, and also, as a professor of law at the College of William & Mary. During the Revolutionary days, the Wythe House was used first by French allies, and then by Count Rochambeau. Wythe and his wife had already traveled to Philadelphia for the Constitutional Convention, where they were inoculated against smallpox—a deadly disease with an equally harrowing inoculation process—which shows Wythe's dedication, much like his student and then colleague Thomas Jefferson, to the principles and practices of science and experimentation. Wythe's books and physics instruments were burned in 1781, when parts of Williamsburg and the College of William & Mary were caught in the cross fire of the Revolutionary War.

Colonial Williamsburg interprets the George Wythe House today both from the perspective of Wythe, an elite white plantation owner, scholar, and teacher, as well as from the perspective of the enslaved men and women who labored for him. While Wythe was a Revolutionary, his approach to the "peculiar institution" (the euphemism used to describe slavery in the Southern states) was not. Before his untimely death, Wythe manumitted his enslaved housemaid and cook Lydia Broadnax, and he also showed interest in others, but he did not believe in freeing large swaths of the enslaved populations in Virginia—most whites were afraid that large numbers of freed African Americans would cause chaos or worse, retribution. Wythe's papers were lost after his death; therefore, knowing all of the intricacies of his thinking is not possible. The George Wythe House explores some of these problems in its interpretive work, thus the house goes beyond the usual historic house tour, which used to focus on the decorative arts and Wythe's famous social circle.

When Wythe died under mysterious circumstances—he was poisoned along with two others, but lived long enough to change his will and tell others who he thought committed the crime—his funeral was the largest in Virginia state history to that time. His funeral was at the Virginia State Capitol (there is a marble bust of him there—don't forget to look for it when you visit that National Historic Landmark), and he was buried at St. John's Episcopal Church in Richmond. His sister's grandson, George Wythe Sweeney, whom he took in and taught, was suspected of using arsenic to poison the strawberries at breakfast. He was acquitted at trial—because people of color, who had seen Sweeney act suspiciously—were not allowed to testify.

Hampton Institute (Hampton University)
100 Cemetery Rd., Hampton; (757) 727-5000; hamptonu.edu/
visitor; open for touring and campus visits year-round; free

Founded in 1868 to educate newly freed African Americans after the Civil War, the Hampton Institute is one of the leading HBCUs—historically black colleges and universities—in the US. Hampton Normal and Agricultural Institute was founded a little more than 150 years ago by the American Missionary Association. A 27-year-old Union Army brigadier general, Samuel Chapman Armstrong, became its first leader. With only 2 teachers, 15 students, and little money, Armstrong's educational philosophy for the school was "Education for Life" by providing a program intended to train "the head, the hand, and the heart." This approach was developed by Armstrong after watching his father, a missionary/teacher in the Polynesian Islands (later Hawaii). Union officers provided funds to the school, and Hampton was constructed on a former plantation known as "Little Scotland," in close proximity to Fort Monroe, noted as a center of safety for fleeing enslaved people during the Civil War. Armstrong's idea for a school was preceded by the work of a missionary teacher named Mary Smith Peake, who began teaching the enslaved community in secret under an oak tree.

In 1929 Hampton Institute became a college, and many new programs were added, including library science. The core of the school was as a "normal school," which is the traditional phrase that indicates a school that trains teachers. This continued throughout the 20th century, as Hampton taught its students "agriculture, home economics, education, business, building, librarianship and music"—all with

the intent that students would become professionals within their disciplines. This was certainly the case with Booker T. Washington, who came to Hampton in 1872. At age 25 the young graduate was asked to start the Tuskegee Institute by Armstrong. Some of the more traditional programs such as agriculture were phased out over time in favor of new programs centered around STEM (shorthand today for Science, Technology, Engineering, and Math), which is a huge draw for students in the 21st century.

Hampton Institute has much to see, including Virginia's oldest museum, which contains more than 9,000 artifacts and is the oldest museum of African-American history and culture in the US. Like the College of William & Mary, Hampton Institute had a program within the school to "teach" Native Americans. This amounted to little more than the removal of language and culture for the idea of total assimilation into white American society, and the program was closed in 1923. Information about this program, versions of which occurred all over the country, can be seen in the museum. The visitor center at Hampton Institute provides a free walking tour guidebook called "Family Tree Heritage Sites" that tracks various sites of interest on campus. This includes the Memorial Chapel, the Booker T. Washington Memorial (the school's most famous alumnus), Emancipation Oak, and Hampton National Cemetery. The Emancipation Tree was the site of the first reading of the Emancipation Proclamation in 1863 and has since become a symbol not only for the university, but for Hampton City itself. National Geographic called the oak one of the "ten greatest trees in the world."

James Semple House
Frances St. (south side) between Blair and Walker Sts., Williamsburg; interior not open to the public, exterior available for viewing year-round

Although the James Semple House is not open to the public at Colonial Williamsburg, the house is available for viewing from the outside and is always on the must-see list for scholars and students of Thomas Jefferson, the nation's only architect/president. Although the original construction documents no longer exist, the form of the building, an early and restrained Classicism, has been compared to Monticello (phase one), which was designed by Jefferson in much the same time period. Jefferson was living in Williamsburg during this time, and is therefore thought to have provided a plan to the original owner. The house was later purchased in 1801 by James Semple, a judge and professor of law at the College of William & Mary, thus acquiring the name that has stayed intact for the past two centuries.

Thomas Jefferson's accomplishments outside of architecture mean that for most his drafting of the Declaration of Independence, or involvement with the Louisiana Purchase, or founding of the University of Virginia, supersedes his architectural contributions to the new country. Only when visiting his homes Monticello and Poplar Forest (see separate entries) does this important aspect of his life come into focus—thanks to bricks and mortar. But Jefferson designed several buildings in Virginia, including the State Capitol (see separate entry) and even made alterations to the White House in Washington, D.C. Since elite men of Virginia knew each other—and knew each other's talents—it is no surprise that Jefferson was asked to provide the plans for new buildings, including houses for his friends and acquaintances. Jefferson was enamored of the Classical style, especially as translated through the work of Andrea Palladio, an Italian architect whose work traveled to the US via architectural pattern books.

The James Semple House is called a "Roman country house" in the Palladian style. It has a center block accompanied by two wings on each side. But unlike his own homes in the countryside of Albemarle and Bedford Counties, this was a townhouse for an urban area and was built of timber frame with clapboard sheathing. The facade of the house features a turned roofline, so the gable end forms a pediment when looking straight on—a reference to Classicism, reinforced in white paint, which replicates the idea of marble or limestone, the chosen building materials of the ancient world. There are Doric columns under the portico, which again points to the restrained Classicism of the building—the Doric architectural style is plain, topped with capitals without decoration.

The John Semple House was the residence of John Tyler (of Sherwood Forest Plantation fame, see separate entry), the 10th president of the US who lived here while studying at the College of William & Mary, just as Thomas Jefferson and James Monroe had done. Tyler actually lived here as a boy through young adulthood, because he was a relation to the Semple family and was sent to Williamsburg from the country for his education. For all of these reasons, the James Semple House was known to be a special building when the Colonial Williamsburg Foundation began its work, and it was one of the first buildings to be restored. The house received National Historic Landmark designation in 1970 and continues to be employed for residential use by organization administrators.

John Tyler House (Sherwood Forest Plantation)
14501 John Tyler Memorial Hwy., Charles City; (804) 829-5377; sherwoodforest.org; house tours available, call ahead to arrange; self-guided grounds tours available daily; admission charged

There are a lot of "firsts" or "bests" noted in Virginia history through the National Historic Landmarks program. At Sherwood Forest Plantation, John Henry Tyler's house is known to be the longest frame house in the US. But you can also assign Tyler a secondary superlative: The 10th president of the US fathered 15 children, besting all other American presidents by at least a few (his first wife Letitia bore him eight children, while his second wife, Julia, had seven). Tyler purchased the house from his predecessor, William Henry Harrison, who died in office. The house was constructed in parts over a series of decades. The wood-framed two-story house with dormer windows grew at both ends with dependencies, which were then connected. Then Tyler tacked on a final 68-foot-long structure on the end: a ballroom for dancing the Virginia Reel, popular in the 19th century. The central portion of the house was built in 1720, but by 1780 the structure stretched 300 feet—longer than a football field. Tyler renamed the house and plantation Sherwood Forest, thinking himself as "outlawed" by his political rivals.

The house originally began life as a standard Georgian, but when architectural styles changed, so too did facades of buildings. During the final renovation of the house, Tyler, with second wife Julia Gardiner Tyler, had the house Greek Revivalized. To turn a Georgian or Federal-style house into the stylish Greek Revival, homeowners could hire an architect to add columns, pilasters, cornices, and other touches onto the historic core. White paint was used to replicate the white marble of

ancient temples such as the Parthenon at Athens. According to the current owners of Sherwood Forest, who continue to live on-site, by attaching the work spaces to the main house via colonnades, the kitchen could be placed far from the best room in the house. This attenuated pattern is referred to as "Big House, Little House, Colonnade, Kitchen" and can be seen in many houses across Virginia—even Mount Vernon has such a colonnade connecting the house to the service wing.

Tyler had a long political career. After serving in the US House of Representatives and the Senate, he was vice president when Harrison died in office—the first time this happened in the US—and a year later his wife died. Earning the ignominious moniker the "accidental president," Tyler presided over the years preceding the secession of the South, an environment increasingly ripe for Civil War. He tried working for peace between North and South, but it was futile. After finishing his three-year term, Tyler was not nominated to run for president, but his political career was not quite over—he became a member of the government of the Confederate States of America. But he died only a year into the war. Because of Tyler's younger second wife, two of his grandsons are still alive and retain ownership of Sherwood Forest, well into the 21st century!

Peyton Randolph House
100 W. Nicholson St., Williamsburg; (888) 965-7254; colonial williamsburg.com/locations/peyton-randolph-house; open year-round except Mon, Wed, and Fri; Colonial Williamsburg ticket needed to enter

Virginia is filled with National Historic Landmarks dedicated to the men of the American Revolution. As a large state, Virginia had seven signers of the Declaration of Independence, not to mention the man who wrote it, and the man who led the army in ensuring the ideas in the document became a material reality. Each of the houses of these men has been saved, and all are National Historic Landmarks. But there were many more Revolutionaries in this historical mix—both men and women, black and white—whose names are not known beyond state boundary lines, and perhaps not even past the Williamsburg Historic District area. George Wythe (1726–1806) and Peyton Randolph (1721–1775) are such people. Randolph might have been more well-known if he had lived through the American Revolution. Dying the year before the Declaration of Independence was signed, a months-long process presided over by John Hancock in the Continental Congress, Randolph was the first and second president of that Congress in 1774 to 1775.

Randolph's house, a unique Georgian-era timber-framed house, was built over three successive phases, starting about 1715. This makes the house one of the oldest surviving buildings in the Williamsburg Historic District and a unique one, in terms

of its long facade, red paint color, and the fact that unusually—as a house made of wood—much of the material is original, because the house never suffered a fire. Randolph's father lived in the house first, and Peyton inherited it and lived here from 1745 to 1775. Randolph served as speaker for the Virginia House of Burgesses for nine years before going to Philadelphia for the first Continental Congress. His time spent in the Virginia legislature prepared him well for working with the elite men from across the 13 colonies as they determined their grievances toward King George III of England and made preparations for separating themselves from the most powerful empire in the world.

During the Revolution, the Peyton Randolph House served the Comte de Rochambeau in the Yorktown campaign, and many men of Virginia, including George Washington, Thomas Jefferson, and George Wythe visited here. The Marquis de Lafayette, returning to the US in 1826 for his "farewell tour" and to celebrate the 50th anniversary of the Declaration of Independence, also stayed here, making the Peyton Randolph House, once again, the center of social life in Williamsburg. The first construction of the house was actually square in shape, but with two additions—one a stand-alone two-story structure to the east in 1724, and the other a final connection between the two buildings—the house became an elongated structure, with all additions likely completed by Peyton Randolph himself. Randolph inserted wood paneling in this third section with bay windows, which created the long facade seen today. As with many Virginia houses, the Peyton Randolph House was not untouched by the Civil War. By the 1860s the house was owned by the Peachy family and was used as a hospital for Union and Confederate troops wounded during the Battle of Williamsburg on May 5, 1862. The house became a National Historic Landmark in 1970, not long after Colonial Williamsburg finished its restoration in 1968.

Shirley Plantation
501 Shirley Plantation Rd., Charles City; (804) 829-5121; shirley plantation.com; guided tours available daily 9:30 a.m. to 4:30 p.m.; admission charged

The Commonwealth of Virginia—a term interchangeable with the word *state* but purposefully connoting a direct connection to the welfare of the people—has a series of scenic byways marked with small blue signs featuring the state bird (cardinal) and flower (flowering dogwood). On State Route 5 between Richmond and Williamsburg is a scenic byway that travels along the north bank of the James River, passing through three of the original eight "shires" (or counties) of the Colony of Virginia. This includes Henrico County, Charles City County, and James City County. Out of the nine plantations that can be seen while driving the byway, four are National Historic Landmarks—indicating the deep, rich history of Virginia, pertinent to the development of the colonies and to the US. King Charles I of England created these shires out of the Colony of Virginia in 1613, hence the reason one of the areas was named for him. Things didn't turn out well for Charles—he was beheaded in 1649—but the county named for him and plantations within go on, 400 years later.

Shirley is, then, the oldest working plantation in the US. Currently the 11th generation of the family continues the "family business" of Shirley, including keeping the house open for tours. The first house at Shirley is no longer extant, but the

second house, built from 1723 to 1738, has the stamp of being a related to Robert "King" Carter, the wealthiest man in Virginia. When Carter died he left 300,000 acres, 1,000 enslaved people, and 10,000 British pounds to his family. He was a king in all but name! His eldest son John—remember primogeniture in play, meaning the eldest son inherited the best/most of any estate unless otherwise determined—married Elizabeth Hill, and the house at Shirley was their wedding gift. Today the Hill Carter descendant families keep the house intact, which includes decorative arts such as portraits, silver, furniture, and ceramics.

As with many plantation houses of the pre-Revolutionary period, the Georgian style was generally utilized in the colonies, but often with unique adaptations. Case in point for Shirley: a "flying staircase"—where the underside of a staircase seems to float in midair—and a Queen Anne–styled forecourt (the only remaining example of this architectural style in North America) are worth noting. Virginia, again due to its age and wealth, is a primary source for learning about the beginning of cultural history in the US. Some of the names and events associated with the plantation beyond those first mentioned include the Marquis de Lafayette, whose troops used Shirley for a supply depot and listening post during the Revolutionary War; George B. McClellan, who issued a safeguard against any harm coming to Shirley, since the women of the house were tending wounded soldiers; Robert E. Lee, whose parents, Anne Hill Carter Lee and Gen. Henry Lee, were married in the parlor in 1793; and Harry Washington, not famous, but known to be a young man enslaved at Shirley who ran away in 1863 to join the Union Army.

On the tour you can see formal gardens and eight original outbuildings. But the most telling feature of the house may not be the house itself, but the distance from the James River to the house. A horse and carriage took visitors to the house, wrapping around it to drop visitors at the entrance to the Great Hall.

Westover Plantation

7000 Westover Rd., Charles City; (804) 829-2882; westover-plantation.com; open daily 10 a.m. to 5 p.m.; admission charged for private house tour, schedule in advance; admission to the grounds and gardens $5 (honor system)

It's easy to imagine the importance of rivers to people living in the Tidewater—whether they were Native American, British subjects, or the first generations of Americans—by spending time at Westover, a plantation house built only 150 feet from the James River. For the past (almost) three hundred years, that proximity meant ease of access to a transportation network and a splendid view from both the water and from the house. In the 21st century, though, the relationship to changing weather patterns and rising waters may mean something very different for Westover—in 2003, for example, the embankment was significantly eroded during a hurricane and a historic road partially washed into the James. Belonging to the coterie of James River Plantations, Westover sits on a spit of land surrounded by the James River to the south and Herring Creek to the north and east. Berkeley Plantation is close by.

Built in the mid-18th century—there has been a resetting of the earlier date of 1730 to the more current 1750—Westover Plantation was the seat of the William Byrd II family, which built its wealth first in tobacco, the further purchase and cultivation of land, and political appointments and work. The house and plantation were serviced by more than 200 enslaved people, first working tobacco and then

replacement cash crops such as wheat. Byrd founded Richmond, which he named for Richmond-upon-Thames in England—he had spent his youth in England, only returning to the colony upon his father's death.

The Georgian style of Westover is typical—you can recognize the telltale signs now from your National Historic Landmark visits. A central rectangular block with a hipped roof and chimneys, accompanied by two buildings at each side, give the house a grand size and an imposing structure. Symmetry is the main thing about Georgian architecture (named, of course, for the king Georges in power in England during the long 18th century), but there is also a refined and restrained exterior decoration, balanced on the interior by richly decorated ceilings in plasterwork and displays of wealth through the decorative arts, the color of paint used on the walls, and the hand-planed architectural moldings around windows, doorways, and archways. But, there are details to notice special only to Westover: three original wrought iron gates outside were imported from England, a still existing underground tunnel which runs from the house to the riverbank—not an uncommon feature for homes with direct connections to trade and transport—and the deeply carved doorway which frames entrance to the house. The so-called "Westover" door is heavily carved with a broken pediment over two fluted pilasters with Corinthian style capitals. In the center top is a pineapple, a symbol of hospitality repeated in the ironwork gate finials. Doorways such as this are considered by many to be works of art in their own right, as they are really a form of high-relief sculpture.

On a sunny Virginia day, there's much to occupy your time at Westover Plantation. The Byrds are buried here, and you can see William Byrd II's elaborate, but very

weathered obelisk-styled gravestone. The current owners of Westover encourage use of the grounds. Dogs are welcome on a leash, and picnics can be brought in to enjoy while watching the James River continue its journey to the Chesapeake Bay.

Williamsburg Historic District
101 Visitor Center Dr., Williamsburg; (888) 965-7254; colonial williamsburg.com/historic-area; open year-round with different ticket/tour options available

Williamsburg is many things. It is one of the early Virginia plantations in the Tidewater (founded in 1636 as the Middle Plantation); it is home to the country's second-oldest institution of higher learning, the College of William & Mary (a National

Historic Landmark described next); it is home to Colonial Williamsburg, a nearly 100-year-old re-created and restored living history museum spread across 301 acres; and it is a traditional vacation paradise for individuals and families who enjoy a mix of history and entertainment: in addition to Colonial Williamsburg, Busch Gardens

is here, as well as easy access to the other attractions in the Historic Triangle, which includes Historic Jamestown and Yorktown.

Within this bustling city (and *city* is a relative term—in Virginia, Williamsburg is structured as an independent city, even though there are just over 14,000 residents—not quite the same idea of a city that other states might have!) are plentiful shopping, dining, and natural area experiences. Also within the city is Williamsburg Historic District, which is the core of the not-for-profit called the Colonial Williamsburg Foundation. Called Williamsburg for short, the historic district is centered around the Duke of Gloucester Street, radiating out in different directions on streets filled with colonial American architecture. Shortened to "DoG" Street, this 99-foot-wide dirt road is lined with colonial-era shops, taverns, and a visitor center. At one mile long, the east end of DoG Street ends with the reconstructed Capitol, while the west end of the street ends at Merchants Square, a contemporary outdoor shopping plaza created out of a Colonial Revival streetscape built in the 1920s and 1930s (and where you can pose with a seated bronze statue of Thomas Jefferson writing the Declaration of Independence). This project, spearheaded by W.A.R. Goodwin, coincided with the impact and investment of John D. Rockefeller, Jr. who began the work to restore and re-create the historic district of Williamsburg into "Colonial Williamsburg" in 1926. DoG Street is closed to traffic, but, when walking here you will often find other modes of transportation—costumed interpreters on horseback and visitors riding in horse and carriage around the historic district are common sights.

Many people still live today within the Williamsburg Historic District, so the area takes on a residential feel in addition to its daily use as an educational and tourism entity. As a visitor you are free to walk DoG and surrounding streets for free, but to enter the historic house museums you must purchase a ticket. Williamsburg

is known for its dedication to education and interpretation, and staff appear in colonial-era costumes, sometimes taking on the role of particular historic persons who lived, studied, or worked here in the 18th century. Because Williamsburg was the capital of Virginia after moving from Jamestown (and before moving to Richmond), political life and discussions are always part of the mix. Thomas Jefferson,

James Madison, and George Washington often appear in the Historic District, as do Patrick Henry, the Marquis de Lafayette, George Mason, and a crew of "Nation Builders": costumed interpreters who represent the lives of people whose names might be forgotten today, but played important roles in the pre-Revolutionary era. This includes African Americans such as James Armistead Lafayette, Edith Cumbo, and the Rev. Gowan Pamphlet.

Williamsburg is a National Historic Landmark District in its own right, but within the area are buildings with individual National Historic Landmark status, including the Wren Building at the College of William & Mary and Bruton Parish Church (the oldest continually operating church in the US), as well as the Peyton Randolph House, the George Wythe House, and the James Semple House (all with separate entries).

Wren Building, College of William & Mary

**111 Jamestown Rd., Williamsburg; (757) 221-1540; wm.edu/
about/history/historiccampus/wrenbuilding/index.php; academic
building still in use, visitors welcome outside of classroom use**

Harvard claims status as the oldest university in the American Colonies (1636) and rival Yale University comes as third oldest (1701), but between the two northern institutions is William & Mary, a research university in the Virginia public higher education system. Founded in 1693, William & Mary is located close to Colonial Williamsburg and Merchants Square, making a walk today between these three areas a step back in time, with plenty of educational experiences to round out the

shopping and eating. Named for English royalty, King William III and Queen Mary II, the school's heritage is unlike that of Harvard and Yale, which were founded as theological seminaries.

In its time the Wren Building was one of the largest brick buildings constructed in the colonies in the 18th century. The cornerstone was laid soon after the school's founding, and the building has been in continual use ever since, making it the oldest educational building extant and working well into the 21st century. With four stories, lecture space, refectory (dining room), a long gallery for hanging portraits, and a chapel (added later), the Wren Building provides a glance into education for elite males in the colonies—an education intended for people like Thomas Jefferson and James Monroe, who both studied here. The Wren Building, combined with the President's House and the Brafferton (a house constructed for the Indian School), comprise what is called the "Ancient Campus" at William & Mary, the heart of the school.

Named a National Historic Landmark in 1960 (like so many others in this book—there must be a story behind that year and its bumper crop of nominations to the program), the building has undergone several major restorations, like everything located in Williamsburg. Most colonial buildings—whether brick or timber frame—have suffered the ravages of time, due to lack of maintenance but also due to destruction by fire. And, in the case of a building like the Wren, with a long history, there have been not just one fire, but several, occurring in different eras—1705, 1859, and 1862—resulting in different approaches to preservation and restoration over time. The Wren Building thus presented a great challenge to the generations of preservationists intent on stabilizing the building in the 20th century, part of the larger campaign to restore the Williamsburg historic area. The Wren Building always received special attention from architectural historians of Virginia and

philanthropists such as John D. and Abby Aldrich Rockefeller due to its age, but also due to the name associated to the building. The Wren Building is named for Sir Christopher Wren, the well-known architect of St. Paul's Cathedral in London. It is believed that though Wren did not visit the colonies or Virginia, he did provide the plan for the building, making it the only Wren building in the Western Hemisphere.

On the top of the building is a weather vane with the year 1693 cut into the banner-shaped metal. Although today considered a masterpiece of Colonial architecture utilizing the Flemish bond style—a fancy form of brickwork—Thomas Jefferson detested going to school here, claiming the buildings and campus were crowded and not suitable for a thoughtful educational experience. Compare your visit to the Wren Building to your visit to the Rotunda on the University of Virginia campus. How did Jefferson's three years here inform his designs for the public university he founded nearly a century later? A visit to the rear exterior of the building will provide you with a list of William & Mary firsts—including status as the first college to have an intercollegiate fraternity, Phi Beta Kappa, formed December 5, 1776 (apparently other things happened that momentous year!).

HEART OF APPALACHIA

Pocahontas Exhibition Coal Mine
(Pocahontas Coal Mine Exhibition and Museum)
215 Shop Hollow Rd., Route 659, Pocahontas; (276) 945-9522; dmme.virginia.gov/dmme/dapocahontas.shtml; open Apr through Oct; admission charged

Virginia's listing of National Historic Landmarks does not have many sites to visit associated with labor history; therefore a trip to the Pocahontas Exhibition Coal Mine, also called Pocahontas Mine No. 1, is a chance to experience through sight, smell, and sound what turn-of-the-20th-century coal mining was like for thousands of Americans across the Appalachians. Opening in 1882 in the Pocahontas Coalfield, a rich field of quality semi-bituminous coal, the mine became a tourist attraction of sorts 50 years later. Coal mining changed considerably by the mid-20th century, and in 1955 Pocahontas closed for active mining. In the glorified age of the automobile, when it was possible to drive through carved-out giant redwoods in California, climb to the top of Mount Washington in New Hampshire, and hit diners along Route 66, Pocahontas reopened instead for drive-through touring, which lasted until 1970.

Pocahontas was a successful mine, especially for producing coke, which was used in steel production. Skyscrapers and building construction across the country needed steel in the 20th century, but so did the US military. Fighting two world wars necessitated the acquisition of much material, including coke and coal, and the US Navy was able to take advantage of the Virginian location of Pocahontas by shipping these materials across the state by Norfolk & Western Railroad to Norfolk. The smokeless quality of Pocahontas coal was an advantage to naval warfare, giving the US and its allies a distinct advantage. Several other mines opened in the area, due to the ease of access to the seam of coal in the landscape, the train line that serviced the area, and the need for coal and steel during the age of modern architecture and warfare.

Located less than one mile from the West Virginia state line, the coal mine also supported various businesses in the area in the 20th century, including multiple machine shops to service the mining equipment. The hilly Appalachian landscape is, of course, dissected by rivers, streams, and creeks, and thus Pocahontas was built close to multiple water sources, including Laurel Fork and the Coal Branch stream. Dumping from mines such as Pocahontas created huge piles of waste material, as high as 100 feet. Today much of the area has been reclaimed by nature, but there are three structures still on-site to view and visit, including Virginia's Official Coal Heritage Museum. Because Pocahontas Mine No. 1 was such an important center for coal production—by 1955 more than 44,000,000 tons—Pocahontas was declared a National Historic Landmark in 1994. In 2018 the site was closed for renovation and refurbishment, and the current managers of Pocahontas, the Virginia Department of Mines, Minerals and Energy, welcomed visitors back in 2019.

NORTHERN VIRGINIA

Alexandria Historic District
Alexandria City; (Visitor center: 221 King St., Alexandria, VA 22314; 703-838-5005 or 800-388-9119); visitalexandriava.com/ old-town-alexandria

The Alexandria Historic District is known as "Old Town Alexandria," a National Historic Landmark designated area within a city on the west bank of the Potomac River. Laid out in a grid in the 18th century, Old Town Alexandria has everything a lover of culture would want in a weekend's visit: historic houses, art centers, diverse restaurants, and access to waterfront parks for walking. Old Town Alexandria has a sophisticated air about it due to the city's close location—only five miles—to Washington, D.C., and its Northern Virginia environs. But this contemporary flair rests on a solid core of early Americana, the reason for its National Historic Landmark designation. Sites to see outside of the National Historic Landmarks include the not-to-be-missed Carlyle House, the Torpedo Factory Art Center (inside you can visit artists in their studios at work, but on the third floor is also the Alexandria Archaeology Museum), and the Stabler-Leadbeater Apothecary Museum, where Martha Washington used to obtain medicines. It's possible to shop and dine to your heart's content in Old Town Alexandria, but visitors come for the atmosphere— row houses with brightly painted doors, many displaying American flags, are the norm, and many of the houses keep old-style flame-like lanterns lit. Take a walk

during the early evening, on the uneven cobblestones, and you might think you've been transported to the past. Just maybe, if you turn a corner, you might come across some American Revolutionaries visiting Gadsby's Tavern for their evening meal and a conversation about taxes!

One of those early Revolutionaries was George Washington, who came to Alexandria as a surveyor and eventually returned as a president. Alexandria became a wealthy seaport town, serving the interests of Northern Virginia, which accounts for the density of Federal-style houses. But the city also has surviving waterfront warehouses that today hold shops and businesses, rather than tobacco and grain—the major commodities and products of Virginia until the late-20th century (soybeans rule the landscape today).

Ball's Bluff Battlefield Historic District (part of Ball's Bluff Regional Park and National Cemetery)

Ball's Bluff Rd., Ball's Bluff Battlefield Regional Park and National Cemetery, Leesburg; (703) 737-7800; novaparks.com/parks/balls-bluff-battlefield-regional-park; open every day from dawn to dusk for self-guided tours, visitor center open Apr through Nov; free

In a state with iconic names of Civil War battlefields such as Chancellorsville, Manassas, Fredericksburg, and Spotsylvania, Petersburg and Appomattox come easily to mind. Smaller battlefields such as Ball's Bluff, Cedar Creek, or Five Forks (see

separate entries for each) are less well-known, but each has an important piece of the story to tell—and thus were given National Historic Landmark status. Ball's Bluff, on the Potomac River in Northern Virginia, is both a battlefield site and a national cemetery, although one of the smallest in the country. A cemetery is located here for 54 Union soldiers in 25 gravesites—markers on the landscape remind visitors of the toll of war, but also of individual lives lost, despite the fact that all but one of the burials are of unknowns. The Battle of Ball's Bluff on October 21, 1861, although a small conflict, was another defeat early in the war for the Unionists, but also the death scene for one of Abraham Lincoln's personal friends, US Senator Col. Edward D. Baker. The senator was killed here, along with more than 200 others, and another 226 were wounded. Union soldiers were driven over the bluff and forced to swim the Potomac River, where many of them died, their bodies floating downstream. The rest of the men—more than 500—surrendered rather than drown. There are monuments to Baker and Confederate Sergeant Clinton Hatcher close by, although neither man is buried here.

Battles are fought on the ground, but they are also fought in the halls of government. The Battle of Ball's Bluff was a military defeat, but the way it changed the American way of making war during the Civil War era is the subtle reason for its National Historic Landmark status. After the battle, concerns about the loyalties of some members of the military was questioned, leading to the creation of the Joint Committee on the Conduct of the War, which was empowered to investigate the actions of individual officers. Proceedings undertaken by this committee led to myriad problems, including the potential to destroy military officers' careers, but at the same time also offered a unique glance into the decisions and actions made during many of the most important battles in Virginia. Questions about the separation of powers by succeeding American leaders during times of war would reference this event and its aftermath.

Ball's Bluff Battlefield is almost wholly unchanged since the late 19th century, and for that reason, too, became a National Historic Landmark in a larger regional park. The landmark's place inside a larger NOVA Parks site provides a robust interpretive experience—volunteer-led tours are offered on the weekend in two lengths (short tour is 40 minutes, and a longer, in-depth tour is 90 minutes), but be prepared for moderately strenuous walking. To visit Ball's Bluff you need to walk the bluff!

Belmont, Gari Melchers Home & Studio
224 Washington St., Falmouth; (540) 654-1015; garimelchers.org; open daily 10 a.m. to 5 p.m.; admission charged

This historic site is a standout in the National Historic Landmarks program in Virginia, because it is the only site dedicated to an American artist. Owned in the early 1900s by the renowned American artist Gari Melchers (1860–1932), this historic house is handsomely furnished with items collected during the family's life and travels abroad. Although not a household name today in the same way that Andrew Wyeth is, Melchers was a distinguished landscape and portrait painter of his time, and his home is a time capsule of sorts for the Gilded Age in a state known more for its Revolutionary-era buildings and stories or the Civil War. Melchers's home, which he called Belmont, was in origins a Georgian-period house, adapted and updated with features common to the turn of the 20th century. Like many wealthy Americans who could afford a "retreat" or country house, Gari and his wife Corinne chose a house on a picturesque ridge overlooking the Rappahannock River, surrounded by the shade of woodland trees and shrubs.

Gari Melchers was a well-known artist and art teacher, completing murals such as *Peace and War* for the Library of Congress in Washington, D.C. But it seems the artist was also a romantic. While both he and a young artist named Corinne were traveling on an ocean liner, they met and fell in love. They lived primarily in New York and traveled abroad extensively, collecting decorative arts and other materials for their homes, including Belmont, which they purchased in 1916. The house had already been in existence for more than 100 years and had been enlarged before the Civil War, but the Melchers added a hexagonal-shaped sunroom, bathrooms, and even a whole third floor, which gave the Melchers and their guests plenty of space—and also plenty of room to decorate with their European-acquired mix of materials. Those members of American society who could afford to travel and

collect during the Gilded Age, which ended abruptly with World War I in Europe, set their sights on tapestries, ceramics, paintings, candlesticks, silver, furniture, and family heirlooms. There is no other National Historic Landmark in Virginia like Belmont—both the house and the collections within are unique to the people who put the ensemble together.

Corinne lived for 23 years after Gari's death in 1932 and continued to care for his artistic reputation by managing exhibits of his work. When she died in 1955, her ashes were interred with Gari's behind a plaque in a wall of the beautiful studio building. Today the Museum Shop is the official home of the Stafford County Visitor Center, where visitors can find information about Stafford County attractions, restaurants, hotels, and other amenities. The Marguerite Stroh Visitor Center features a museum shop and orientation theater, and 27 acres of grounds, gardens, and guided woodland trails offer access to the Rappahannock through the seasons.

Christ Church (Christ Church Episcopal)
118 N. Washington St., Alexandria; (703) 549-1450; historicchrist church.org; church services occur regularly, but visitors are welcome

Called Christ Church Episcopal, the late Georgian redbrick church sits in the heart of Old Town Alexandria and is an example of Wren-influenced architecture in the British Atlantic world. Begun in 1767, the original architect was Colonel James Wren, a descendant of Sir Christopher Wren of St. Paul's Cathedral in London fame. Many church building projects—especially those of the Gothic style, it seems—took years, if not decades or more, to finish. But the parish church fathers were not pleased with the pace of the basically stalled work at Christ Church,

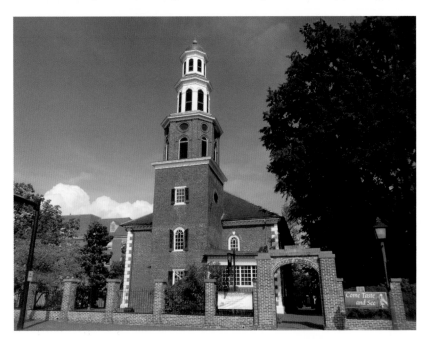

originally called Fairfax Church, and brought in a new man to oversee the project. The church, with its stepped bell tower overlooking Old Town Alexandria, has seen many changes over the course of its more than 250-year history. The church was finished in 1773, three years before the American Revolution, survived the "disestablishment" of the Church of England by the State of Virginia, and was occupied by Union troops during the Civil War,

Although it is easier to think about the presence of slavery in places such as Virginia plantations, Christ Church is a physical monument to the monies generated by the state's wealthy tobacco growers and merchants. The cash raised from so-called "cash crops" like tobacco enabled the Fairfax Vestry to build in fine materials, in a fine style, by a fine architect. The walls of the church were constructed of Flemish bond, a method of brick-building that created a pattern in the walls, and at each end, there are stone quoins painted white to emphasize the outline of the building. Other features are Palladian in nature—a style of architecture made famous by Italian architect Andrea Palladio, whose work was the source for much Neoclassicism in Virginia. This includes a Palladian window, which is a vertical window with a lunette, or moon-shaped window above, and the use of broken pediments, which were popular during the Baroque era in Europe and transferred into the Classicism of Wren.

Because of its location in Alexandria and its European-inspired architecture, Christ Church drew parishioners of the upper classes, including George Washington,

Charles Lee, and his descendant Robert E. Lee (both of Stratford Hall), and in the 20th century, Franklin Delano and Eleanor Roosevelt, who visited with Winston Churchill to commemorate (and pray for, no doubt) peace, in 1942 during World War II. The church remained intact throughout its past 250 years—even during the Civil War, when Union troops often left other churches in ruins, Christ Church was spared. Its interior is original, making it an unusual survivor. Special things to see include the last hand-carved hymnal rack in the Lee family pew (founding families with funds would donate to the church and have access to pews stenciled with their names) and hand-painted tablets on each side of the altar area, which were done by Wren and have never been touched. Outside, a historic cemetery is certainly worth a look for the evocative 19th-century grave markers. There is also a special section for 34 Confederate soldiers reminding visitors that wars were not only fought in rural areas, but, in urban centers, too.

Ferry Farm, George Washington Boyhood Site
268 Kings Hwy., Fredericksburg; (540) 370-0732; kenmore.org/ ff_home.html; tours offered hourly; admission charged

Did George Washington chop down the cherry tree here at his family's plantation called Ferry Farm? Not likely according to historians—the story was invented to illustrate Washington's honesty, devotion to learning moral behavior, and modeling it for others. Although the cherry tree story is a myth, perhaps Washington, as a youth, learned much from watching his father, Augustine Washington, manage multiple business enterprises, including several plantations and a partnership in the Accokeek (Potomac) Iron Furnace. Ferry Farm, on the banks of the Rappahannock River, became Washington's home when he was six and remained his primary residence until adulthood (and thus called the "Home Farm" at the beginning). In the midst of growing up, he lost his father, who died when George was 11. Before his death, Augustine built his family a small house on the bluffs overlooking the Rappahannock. The house was damaged by fire in 1748, but evidence for its size and placement was found by archaeologists in 2008. The historic site is thus undergoing a transformation, as the George Washington Foundation has rebuilt the house and is in the midst of a reinterpretation of the landscape.

Ferry Farm was named for the ferry that crossed the Rappahannock River—a feature used by the Washington family. When the house and landscape were purchased in the late-20th century for preservation, the road to the original ferry site was the only remaining Washington-era feature intact. The rest of the historic buildings were gone, although there was a series of 19th- and 20th-century buildings onsite. Ferry Farm was deemed National Historic Landmark material for its potential archaeological contributions as related to George Washington. Parson Weems, who

wrote the first biography of Washington, presented stories that gave Americans a figure to emulate and admire, but what of Washington's real life and times? Ferry Farm is seen as a historic site that can help visitors get close to understanding a real man beyond the myths. An open-to-visitors archaeological lab, tours of the rebuilt house, and even an iPad tour of the landscape are opportunities for learning provided to visitors. Mary Washington, George's mother (and the second wife of Augustine) lived at Ferry Farm until she went to live with a daughter across the river in Fredericksburg. Her house is open for visitors, too (1200 Charles St., Fredericksburg, Virginia 22401).

But, there is more of Washington to be found in Tidewater, or Eastern Virginia. While he spent his youth and young adulthood at Ferry Farm, Washington was born at Popes Creek in Westmoreland County, Virginia. That site, called the George Washington Birthplace, is not a National Historic Landmark, but it is a National Monument managed by the National Park Service (see nps.gov/gewa/index.htm). Like Ferry Farm, the original Washington-era buildings are gone, but visiting the exhibits and landscape and learning about the "Tidewater Aristocracy" into which he was born, help us understand his worldview and behavior throughout his life.

Franklin & Armfield Office

1315 Duke St., Alexandria; (703) 836-2858; nvulypn.wildapricot .org/Visit-the-Museum; open Mon through Fri 10 a.m. to 4 p.m.; free

Of all of the National Historic Landmark buildings and sites visited for this book, none capture the true horror of slavery the way this nondescript brick townhouse does—once you know the story of what took place here. Although today the building functions as the Freedom House Museum, its location in a much-changed urban area of the city, away from the Old Town with its cobblestone streets and shops, does very little to open the story to visitors and tourists. A Virginia Historical Highway Marker (those are white-painted metal with black lettering) stands in front, but no exterior interpretation or marketing points the way to this site, although the sign says enough: This building was leased by Isaac Franklin and his nephew John Armfield, and from here, they together ran the largest slave trading enterprise in the US from 1828 to 1836. In those years, it is estimated that between 1,000 and 2,000 people per year passed through this office and its pen-holding complex (now destroyed). Ownership of slave ships and location close to the wharves in Alexandria made this geographic location suitable—and profitable.

The institution of slavery made whites wealthy, and this business is a good example of such. Isaac Franklin was able to retire in 1836, because he had made more than half a million dollars—in the mid-19th century, mind you. His role was to sell the enslaved men, women, and children in the Deep South states, people who had been forcibly shipped over the Atlantic to Virginia and then kept in holding pens behind this building. John Armfield managed the administration of the work from here, while Franklin sold the slaves to plantation owners in Louisiana and Mississippi. It is possible to see the way Africans were treated as property by Armfield and Franklin from the Virginia Census in 1830, which lists the gender and age for the people held in their pens:

1 male under 10
50 males 10–24
20 males 24–36
4 females under 10
50 females 10–24
20 females 24–36

Chained together, each summer enslaved people were marched from Virginia through Tennessee to the Deep South for eventual work on cotton plantations. Franklin and Armfield employed agents across the Southern states to help them with local sales. When Franklin and Armfield closed in 1836, the business was sold to other slave traders, and the practice continued until 1861, when, at the beginning of the Civil War, Union troops took over Alexandria and the building was used to

hold Confederate prisoners in the very same pens used for enslaved Africans. After the war, the building became a hospital.

Seldom mentioned in Alexandria's glossy tourism marketing brochures and in the visitor center where the stories of Washington and Revolutionary Old Town reign supreme, the Franklin & Armfield Office building survives as a witness to the second great phase of the American experiment—that of ending what the Founding Fathers knew was, in the words of Thomas Jefferson, a "moral and political depravity." It took four years and more than 620,000 American lives to do so.

Gadsby's Tavern

134 N. Royal St., Alexandria; (730) 746-4242; gadsbytavern.org; restaurant separate; self-guided and guided tours available year-round; museum admission charged

Not the only historic tavern on the National Historic Landmark registry in Virginia (see also the Rising Sun Tavern in Fredericksburg), Gadsby's Tavern is unique for its presidentially heavy history, its companion working restaurant open next door for dining, and the historic icehouse within its basement that can be visited anytime from an exterior viewing window. Located in the heart of Old Town Alexandria, Gadsby's Tavern offers a look into hospitality through the ages, from the first time doors opened in circa 1785 to today, with a menu that reflects American history, culture, and tradition. Located on a busy corner (and thus attractive for travelers coming from two directions), Gadsby's Tavern consists of two redbrick colonial-era attached buildings, both from the late-18th century. The guest list reads like a "Who's Who?" of Revolutionary and Federal-era America. Gadsby's Tavern Museum consists of two buildings, a ca. 1785 tavern and the 1792 City Hotel. The buildings are named for Englishman John Gadsby, who operated them from 1796 to 1808. Gadsby's establishment was a center of political, business, and social life in early Alexandria. The tavern was the setting for dancing assemblies, theatrical and musical performances, and meetings of local organizations.

Visitors to the tavern include, as always, the most famous man of Northern Virginia—George Washington—but Thomas Jefferson, James Madison, John Adams,

and even the Marquis de Lafayette, Washington's close friend, also dined, discussed, and danced here. Washington is the special historic house guest, since Gadsby's hosted the annual "Birthnight Balls" in his honor, and the president attended twice. But Thomas Jefferson also thought of Gadsby's as special place: In Jeffersonian style, this president held his inauguration party here in 1801, although he had visited earlier that year—something only recently discovered when Jefferson's account ledgers were digitized by the New York Public Library. We know from the account book that Jefferson paid $5.50 to sleep one night, and that he likely paid for a second guest. This was considerably more than Benjamin Latrobe, a friend of Jefferson's and a fellow architect, who also visited Gadsby's. For most folks, spending $1.50 for food, beverage, and bed was average.

Although you can still find a few restaurants along the East Coast where servers dress in 18th-century clothing for atmosphere, Gadsby's is the real thing—a restaurant attached to a museum, where scholarship and public programming provide solid information to a curious 21st-century public who might wonder about early American favorites such as oyster loaves, Indian cornbread, and hasty pudding. Gadsby's was and remains a central part of the social, economic, political, and educational life of the city of Alexandria, and it was designated a National Historic Landmark in 1963. Step outside the door and walk around the corner and step down—inserted into the basement of the building is a glass window where visitors can view the historic ice well. This ice well demonstrates the sophistication of Gadsby's Tavern—ice would have been used to serve cool drinks, but also for special new foods constantly being introduced or developed in the US, such as ice cream.

George C. Marshall House
(George C. Marshall International Center)
312 E. Market St., Ste. C, Leesburg; (703) 777-1301; georgecmarshall.org; open year-round except Jan and Feb; admission charged

George C. Marshall is such a large character in 20th-century history that he appears twice in this book. The George C. Marshall Museum and Library, on the campus of the Virginia Military Institute (VMI) in Lexington, Virginia, examines Marshall's youth, career at VMI, and service during World War I. Further, the museum and library hold his papers and artifacts and spend much time on Marshall's impact during World War II and in the postwar period as a statesman. This museum, in Northern Virginia and close to Washington, D.C., was his home during the 1940s and 1950s, which has since been turned into something very different from your typical historic house museum. The George C. Marshall International Center instead focuses on Marshall's legacy and current relevance in our era, the 21st century.

General George Catlett Marshall served in the US military for decades, and thus this was the first house he owned as an adult that he considered to be "home"— although it was really a retreat from Washington life. He lived here with his wife Katherine. The early 19th-century wood-frame house was altered over time and updated to reflect their mid-20th-century tastes, which the museum has worked to restore. It's hard to imagine the impact that one person had on the fate of world history. Marshall is such a person. He was Army chief of staff in 1939, overseeing the growth of the 175,000-man US Army into a fighting force of more than 8 million by war's end. He worked on plans for the Allied invasion of France; knew Roosevelt, Churchill, and Stalin personally; and was a brilliant strategist, administrator, and logistics manager. He was one of the few military leaders to have a postwar career as significant as his wartime work.

Although stationed unsuccessfully in China after the end of the war to help that country unify, Marshall returned home to the US and began drafting a series of aid packages to devastated Europe, known as the Marshall Plan. The work was ultimately successful, providing Europeans with the ways and means to rebuild their countries, stabilize their democracies, and begin to regrow their industries and educational and health systems. Due to this firsthand knowledge of rebuilding efforts, Marshall later was president of the American Red Cross, an organization known for its commitment to alleviating suffering at home, but also abroad. Finally, Marshall, who had helped the Allies see the end of the War in the Pacific in World War II, served as secretary of defense during the first two years of the Korean War (1950–1951).

George C. Marshall died in 1959, and this house passed to other owners. By the 1980s the State of Virginia was experiencing pressures from development growth—a process that continues unabated today. Family farms were split and sold and turned into housing developments, and often old homes were torn down for larger, more modern structures or for retail development. The Marshall house came close to becoming such a casualty, but, as with Thomas Jefferson's home Poplar Forest, a group of local citizens banded together to save the house by raising the funds needed for its purchase and restoration. Today the George C. Marshall International Center offers educational and enrichment programs building on Marshall's extraordinary legacy.

George Washington's Mount Vernon
3200 Mount Vernon Memorial Hwy., Mount Vernon;
(703) 780-2000; mountvernon.org; open daily year-round;
admission charged

In European countries a visitor might go see the mansion house or castle of a king or queen. In African countries perhaps the ancestral land of the same. But in the US, Americans and tourists alike visit the houses of the Founding Fathers and presidents, and reigning supreme over all of them is George Washington and his home and plantation, called Mount Vernon. This Georgian-era mansion with long views

over the Potomac River is as unique as the man himself. The house initiated the historic house preservation movement in the US in the second half of the 19th century, and today it continues to evolve as more archaeology, more architectural restoration, more rebuilding, and fuller educational study and interpretation offer a more robust reading of the man who was "first in the hearts of his countrymen."

Like many Americans since, George Washington felt a deep love for the landscape and his home and, as with Thomas Jefferson, always had one eye focused on his return, despite being called into service by Congress. Although for a brief moment he was offered the opportunity to be king of the new country, he was a republican-styled farmer at heart, writing in 1790, "I can truly say I had rather be at Mount Vernon with a friend or two about me, than to be attended at the seat of government by the Officers of State and the Representatives of every power in

Europe." The home he created for himself, his wife Martha, and her children was the center of his life, a property he inherited when his older brother Lawrence died. More than a hundred enslaved men, women, and children lived at Mount Vernon, too, working the landscape and in the many outbuildings that created a small village on the plantation. Washington tried a number of new methods for agriculturally based product development, including building a gristmill, distillery, and 16-sided treading barn on-site. So, though Washington's presence in uniform (made famous in a full-length portrait by Charles Willson Peale) is the way many think of him, a more accurate image might be that of a tall reserved man on horseback, visiting the various trades and enslaved people working his plantation. This is how he saw himself, as Lin-Manuel Miranda captured so beautifully in the lyrics from *Hamilton*—a phrase based in scripture and that Washington used extensively in his correspondence—"I want to sit under my own vine and fig tree, a moment alone in the shade, at home in this nation we've made."

If you are visiting from afar, Mount Vernon should be given a full day of your time. That way you can have a house tour, visit the outbuildings, walk the landscape, visit the museum exhibitions, visit his and Martha's gravesite as well as a cemetery for the enslaved community, and finally, eat and shop. You won't be the only one there, at any time of the year. Mount Vernon is located only 17 miles from the city named for him (Washington, D.C.), so there are always crowds. But what could be better than learning about a man who could have been king of a new country, yet said with ease, "No thank you"?

George Washington National Masonic Memorial
101 Callahan Dr., Alexandria; (703) 400-4950; gwmemorial.org; open 9 a.m. to 5 p.m. daily, except major holidays; tours daily; admission charged

The area around Northern Virginia—Alexandria, Fredericksburg, and Mount Vernon—is George Washington country. You can create for yourself a George Washington Trail and track down historic sites dedicated to the surveyor turned military commander turned first president, or even hop on the Mount Vernon Trail (nps .gov/gwmp/planyourvisit/mtvernontrail.htm) that connects bikers and walkers in Alexandria to Mount Vernon and vice versa. But this historic site, the George Washington National Masonic Memorial, is unlike anything else you will see—a made-to-be impressive structure on a hill with the stoic face of Washington at the entrance. This place introduces the visitor to an aspect of Washington's life not often discussed: his lifelong membership in the Masons and the way this national and even international group of men honored him.

Although today there are still more than 2 million active Masons in the US, George Washington plays a special role in the American version. Freemasonry dates from the end of the 14th century in Europe, formed around fraternal organizations of stonemasons who cared for each other and performed charitable service (hence the symbol of the square and the compass). Although religion and politics are not formally recognized in Freemasonry, belief in a supreme being and a dedication to ritual around the theme of morality are at the heart of their lodge activities. George Washington was a member and eventual lead of the Lodge of Alexandria, No. 22, which helped him to lay the cornerstone for the US Capitol in 1793. At the ceremony, Washington wore a Masonic apron made for him by the Marquis de Lafayette's wife. Washington took his membership and service in Freemasonry with complete dedication and continued practicing its traditions throughout the Revolutionary War years, during his service to the new US government, and as a retired plantation owner. When he died, Washington was buried with Masonic rites, much as the member of a specific church would be.

The George Washington National Masonic Memorial was constructed in 1932, a project almost a decade in the making. Built to provide Washington's life and service as an example to a country after a world war and in the midst of great cultural change, the memorial is more than a memorial in the traditional sense. While it does have an impressively sized structure modeled on one of the Seven Wonders of the Ancient World—the Lighthouse at Alexandria in Egypt, built on Shooter's Hill overlooking Old Town Alexandria—the memorial is also a building with a series of spaces within to act out the memorializing process by staff and visitors every day. Visitors are allowed on the first and second floors, and there are exhibits, a theater, murals, and statuary galore, as well as a gift shop. Higher levels of the building can be visited with a guided tour, and from the observation deck on the ninth floor, visitors can view the landscape architecture of the Freemason symbol of the square and compass with a large G in the center. G stands for God (also called the "Great Architect"), but in this case the G certainly stands for George, too.

Gerald R. Ford House
514 Crown View Dr., Alexandria; private property, exterior viewing only

This might come as a surprising National Historic Landmark listing, but this nomination indicates how important it is to think beyond the physical structure of any place to the essence of the person who built and/or lived here or did something momentous here. In this case, of course, it is Gerald Rudolph Ford (1913–2006), a politician, statesman, husband, and father. But Ford is really remembered for becoming an American president in a way no one could have guessed—in 1974, Richard

M. Nixon stepped down before he was impeached by Congress, and in doing so, made his vice president ascend to the highest office in the land. And all of that happened here, in this nondescript mid-20th-century suburban house in Alexandria. Ford built this house in 1955 and lived here for the next 20 years, building his family and his career, until that fateful episode that everyone knows today as Watergate, which took down the career of an American president.

Gerald R. Ford was born in Omaha, Nebraska, but grew up in Grand Rapids, Michigan. Though his mother and father were separated and divorced, with Ford changing his name to his stepfather's, he grew up in a loving home, was an Eagle Scout, football star (even turning down offers from the National Football League), and attended both the University of Michigan and Yale Law School. Ford then served in the Navy during World War II and received four awards for his service. At the end of wartime, Ford met Betty Bloomer in Michigan, married, and began his Congressional career as a representative from Michigan, serving the state for 25 years. When Ford became vice president in 1973 due to the resignation of then–Vice President Spiro Agnew, the house had to be refitted for Secret Service needs—including the widening of the driveway to fit the official limousine that would take him to Washington, D.C., and back. In addition, bullet-resistant windows and alarms were installed as well as guard booths in two corners of the yard, and special lighting was placed around the house. It's easy to image neighbors on Crown View Drive watching all of this transformation with awe and perhaps being a little disgruntled due to the interested public that must have driven by often.

Ford, of course, would leave this house in 1974 to reside in the White House, but the house was kept by the Fords until they moved to Denver, Colorado, after Ford's defeat in the presidential election of 1977. Ford doesn't have a strong reputation for his presidential leadership—called the "accidental president," he pardoned Richard Nixon, which was seen poorly at the time; the American economy was in the worst recession since the Great Depression; and the Vietnam War ended, much to the relief, but also humiliation, of the country. But Ford's work in the three years before he lost the presidential election to Jimmy Carter was a balance of some social progress in spite of the many economic and political challenges of a difficult decade.

Gunston Hall
10709 Gunston Rd., Mason Neck; (703) 550-9220; gunstonhall.org; open daily 9:30 a.m. to 5 p.m.; admission charged

Located on the Potomac River only 20 miles south of Washington, D.C., Gunston Hall was George Mason's family home. Framer, or a designer, of the Bills of Rights, Mason is equally remembered in Virginia for his work on the 1776 Virginia Declaration of Rights, which influenced Thomas Jefferson's writing of the Declaration of Independence. Mason built this Potomac River plantation in the mid- to late 1750s, and from the exterior, the redbrick home is unassuming. In truth, Mason's taste was unusual for the period in Virginia, and the interior of Gunston Hall pulls

from different cultural sources, including colonial America's only Chinese-style room; Palladio; the Rococo; and even the Gothic. In this house, Mason and his wife Anne raised nine children (until her death at age 39). He became a leading Revolutionary soon after, traveling to Williamsburg and writing sentences such as, "That all men are born equally free and independent . . .," which were echoed just a few months later by Jefferson.

George Mason's efforts to help shape the ideas and governing laws for a new country extended through wartime. During the years of the American Revolution (1776–1781), Mason served on the Committees of Safety and in the Virginia Assembly. After the fighting ended, there was more work to be done, and Mason again traveled to Philadelphia for the Constitutional Convention. Although he did not sign the final document, objecting to 17 separate issues, Mason watched his work become incorporated by James

Madison into a Bill of Rights, which was adopted in 1791, amending the Constitution. As a Founding Father, Mason is overshadowed by others in his Virginia orbit such as Washington, Jefferson, Madison, and even the volatile Patrick Henry (again, all of whom have houses listed in this book due to the National Historic Landmark status), but it is clear Mason, for whom a state university is named, is a part of this Virginia coterie, which includes great men, great houses, and, always, the incursion of slavery. Mason owned 100 enslaved persons who toiled at Gunston Hall.

When exiting Gunston Hall, you will stand on a unique Gothic-style garden porch and then cross the grass to stand on an artificial viewing platform (an area in the grass), which gives a panoramic view of the river. It's hard to remember today, in the automobile age, but most guests to Gunston Hall in George Mason's time arrived via riverboat—thus the view goes not only from the house to the river, but the river to the house. Although the landscaping of Gunston Hall is a ghost of its former 18th-century self, with remnants of the original geometric garden still seen in a remaining few boxwoods, the allée would have funneled guests directly to the house to meet Mason. Today there remains 550 acres for exploring and walking, including the outbuildings around the house (laundry, kitchen, and a reconstructed schoolhouse). A little further afield, underneath a pathway of fir trees, is the Mason family cemetery.

James Monroe Law Office (The James Monroe Museum)
908 Charles St., Fredericksburg; (540) 654-1043; jamesmonroe museum.umw.edu; open daily; admission charged

A historic property of the University of Mary Washington, the James Monroe Law Office houses the James Monroe Museum, with an array of furnishings, artwork, and personal possessions of Monroe and his family. James Monroe, the fifth president of the US, began his career practicing law in Fredericksburg. The building, which dates to 1815, houses the largest collection of material related to the Virginian, including 1,600 items owned by James and Elizabeth Monroe, 10,000 rare books, and 27,000 documents relating to Monroe, his life, and his legacy and that of his descendants. Unlike Washington, Jefferson, and Madison, who were all buried on the grounds of their homes, Monroe was buried in Richmond (a National Historic Landmark, included in this book), while his house is in Charlottesville (and is not a National Historic Landmark—but visit anyway!). Because Monroe followed his friend Thomas Jefferson so closely, he ended up moving across the state to Albemarle County, living first on land that would become the University of Virginia, and later building a home with his beloved wife Elizabeth in the same Piedmont hills near Monticello. Jefferson said of Monroe, "A better man cannot be."

Among the highlights of museum collections here is the "Monroe Doctrine" desk, where the president is thought to have written the document for which he is most remembered. In his December 2, 1823, address to Congress, President James Monroe articulated the US's policy on the new political order developing in the rest of the Americas and the role of Europe in the Western Hemisphere. The three main concepts of the doctrine—separate spheres of influence for the Americas and Europe, noncolonization, and nonintervention—were designed to signify a clear break between the New World and the autocratic realm of Europe. Although European world powers paid little attention to this statement, the doctrine guided American policy until World War I brought the US back into a militaristic relationship with the world. Another Virginian, Woodrow Wilson, whose home is a National

Historic Landmark and featured in this book, would have a difficult time breaking with the long American tradition of nonintervention, until his hand was forced.

According to the museum, the Monroe Doctrine desk (a "secretary"), dates from circa 1795.

Part of a larger set of furniture purchased by the Monroes while in Paris during Monroe's time as Ambassador to France, the entire set of furniture was brought back to the United States with the family, and accompanied them to the President's House in 1817. Family legend states that this is the desk at which Monroe was sitting when he penned the now famous Monroe Doctrine. The desk also contains a secret compartment, in which a cache of long-forgotten letters was found in the 20th century. The letters were written between Monroe and other notables like Thomas Jefferson and James Madison. They now reside here at the museum in the Ingrid Westesson Hoes Archive.

Like Jefferson and Madison, Monroe was a man of letters. In addition to the desk, Monroe assembled a significant personal library during the course of his lifetime, featuring works on history, philosophy, law, politics, science, military science, religion, and the arts.

Kenmore
1201 Washington Ave., Fredericksburg; (540) 373-3381; kenmore .org; open Mar to Dec; guided house tours only (no self-guided tours); admission charged

With a quick glance, Kenmore seems on the surface to be yet another redbrick Georgian house in Virginia. But there are a few characteristics that make this house worthy of a visit. First, the house is the last surviving structure of a 1,300-acre plantation, which indicates just how quickly towns grew on and around land once cultivated by enslaved laborers. From the exterior view the house is a rather undecorated structure with little to please the eye beyond its symmetry. From the interior perspective the effect is quite different: Rooms on the first floor retain floral plaster decorations in relief, indicating a long tradition from England that was imported to the colonies. The last significant aspect to the house was its ownership: The house was built in 1775 by Colonel Fielding Lewis and his wife Betty Washington, George's sister. Although not called Kenmore until the mid-19th century, when a successive owner named it for his Scottish ancestry, the house is part of the Washington Avenue Historic District and retains a three-acre landscape that features a formal flower garden and that all-time favorite 20th-century planting in Virginia: boxwoods.

The Lewises called the house Millbrook, which makes sense—the rear of the house and property abutted the Rappahannock River, an important feature for any plantation that needed to transport both people and goods to larger cities. While more than 80 people labored outside on the plantation working tobacco, wheat, and corn, the inside of the house benefited from the riches produced by their work: The house is considered the earliest example of a Virginia house having all of its major rooms plastered with design work, including the Great Room, the Library, and the Drawing Room. Tradition states that itinerant craftsmen from France undertook the work and most likely used an architectural pattern book from England for guidance. Thus Kenmore is a physical monument to the relationship between the New World and the Old World. Americans, especially those in Virginia, the first permanent English settlement, utilized European traditions to legitimize their own society and development—a tradition that continued even after the formal break with England.

The house was purchased by the Daughters of the American Revolution in 1922, and today it's managed by the George Washington Foundation, which runs both Kenmore and Ferry Farm, the George Washington boyhood site (see separate entry). A combination ticket to visit both is available, as well as season passes. Given National Historic Landmark status in 1970 for its architectural heritage, Kenmore has an archaeological collection that opens windows into previous centuries. Game pieces such as dominoes, marbles, and dice have been found, in addition to evidence of the efforts of laborers—after Emancipation, Virginia farms were staffed by black Americans who earned "tokens" that were traded in for cash. These small metal stamped tokens—for peeling tomatoes or picking vegetables—were given out at the back door of the house and have been found there in large numbers.

Mount Airy (Mount Airy Farm)
361 Millpond Rd., Warsaw; (804) 333-4930; mountairy.farm; house is private property, but open for tours by reservation only

There are many great Palladian country houses along the Eastern Seaboard of the US, a style especially favored by those living in the Mid-Atlantic States. Pennsylvania has Mount Pleasant in Philadelphia, Maryland has Homewood in Baltimore, and Virginia has Mount Airy in the Northern Neck. There are probably more than a hundred examples of classic Palladian homes in the eastern US, but there are only

a few still in the hands of the original family. Mount Airy, the only National Historic Landmark house with such a pedigree in Virginia, is one of them. That Mount Airy began life as a center for horses—siring, importing, racing, selling—also makes this house unique in the list of Virginia landmarks.

Mount Airy was built along the Rappahannock River by Colonel John Tayloe II and completed in 1764. If you compare the late-medieval Jacobean style of Bacon's Castle against this architectural style of 100 years later, you can easily see the differences. Famous folks of the 17th century came here, including George and Martha Washington and the Marquis de Lafayette and his wife Marie. The Lafayettes would have found Mount Airy's architectural style most appropriate: Palladianism, a form of Neoclassicism, was popular throughout Europe for country house estates and was more tasteful and refined, compared to the outdated and archaic Jacobean style, or the overtly embellished Rococo. Mount Airy features a symmetrical facade, with a projecting arcade under a pediment, hipped roof, and two wings, also called dependencies. Palladianism is the basis for Thomas Jefferson's own brand of Neoclassicism, seen in Monticello and Poplar Forest, both in this book, which follow this pattern. The stonework of the exterior is thought to come from James Gibbs, a practitioner of Neoclassicism in England, whose work would have been known from architectural pattern books.

One of the largest plantations owned by one of the wealthiest Virginians living at the time, Rebecca Tayloe's father presented her and fiancé Francis Lightfoot Lee with 1,000 acres of land, 50 enslaved people, and enough money to fund the construction of their own house, called Menokin (see separate entry). The same architect, William Buckland, who finished the interior of Mount Airy also worked on Menokin. Sandstone located on the Mount Airy plantation provided the building material, and the Lees lived at Mount Airy for two years while Menokin was under construction. Both Francis Lightfoot and Rebecca died in 1797 and are buried here in the Tayloe family cemetery on the grounds of Mount Airy. The historic site received its National Historic Landmark designation due to being the burial site of a signer of the Declaration of Independence, but also because its design is considered the earliest and most complete of expression of Palladianism in the English Colonies.

Today Mount Airy remains a family home, but many parts of the landscape have been turned into an organic farm, wedding venue, and event space, with the hunting grounds available to the public. A bluegrass weekend of music is held at Mount Airy during the warm weather months. The farm and gardens can also be toured, but if you want to see the inside of the house, call ahead to make arrangements.

Potomac Canal Historic District (located within Great Falls Park)
9200 Old Dominion Dr., Great Falls Park, McLean; (703) 285-2965; nps.gov/grfa; open daily except Dec 25; admission charged

This is a place few visitors to Northern Virginia or the nation's capital know about, but, located farther afield, off the beaten path via the George Washington Memorial Parkway, Great Falls Park is a unique natural wonder with layers of cultural meaning grafted onto its waterway. The Potomac River, spelled "Patowmack" in the 18th century, was considered by George Washington to be essential in connecting the Chesapeake Bay to the interior of the young country via a canal system that would allow trade as far west as the Ohio River Valley. Washington developed this idea during his youthful years as a surveyor—he saw these lands and waterways with his own eyes and believed in the potential for economic growth, leading a company of investors beginning in 1784 in the creation of five canals along the Potomac River. These canals needed locks, due to the height changes in geology along the river's path: the Potomac River drops over 600 feet in 200 miles.

Washington's idea was to provide a waterway from the agricultural lands of the interior of the country, passing through the states of Virginia and Maryland, ending up in Chesapeake, and from there, to ports along the Atlantic coastline for global trade. Flatboats were used in this fashion after the canals began opening between 1785 and 1802. To create the canal system, riverbeds were dredged, canals were cut to skirt around falls, and new investors had to be continuously sought, making the project a long one, which eventually clashed with the coming of the steam train age. Great Falls Park is located here because this area contains an area of the river that drops 80 feet in less than a mile. For visitors today these falls provide plenty of picturesque viewing from the safety of the shore. For the canal engineers of the turn of the 19th century, this project, recognized as a feat of early American engineering, must have been a constant struggle—the canal at Great Falls took 17 years to build and contributed to the bankruptcy of the Patowmack Company.

Purchase a ticket in the visitor center and then head out to find the Potomac Canal Historic District, which contains the massive shaped walls of the locks, which you can walk through. Although today it is the roaring, fast-moving water of the Potomac that captures visitors' attention, the remnants of the canal and lock system are reminders of the many ways in which Americans sought to work with nature for economic development. While in use the canals allowed for the transport of agricultural goods such as flour, corn, whiskey, furs, tobacco, and timber. Boatmen would push the flatboats—75 feet long, with pointed ends—along the river, navigate through canals, sell their goods at ports, then sell the wood of their boats and walk back home!

Rising Sun Tavern
1306 Caroline St., Fredericksburg; (510) 373-5630; washington heritagemuseums.org; tours offered daily; admission charged

Outside of Alexandria is Fredericksburg, a historic Virginia city on the banks of the Rappahannock River. Here there are more historic sites to visit with ties to George Washington and his family, including an apothecary, the home of Mary Washington (George's mother, and thus a woman considered special to the country), a historic house, and a tavern. One of four historic sites in the Washington Heritage Museums area, the Rising Sun Tavern is the only one with National Historic Landmark status, generated due to its authentic character and association to Washington: His younger brother, Charles, built this structure in 1760 as a home. In this first incarnation of the life of the house, due to its geographic location and association to the commander of the Continental Army (yes, Washington of course!), famous folks of the Revolution used the home for meetings and a place to stop over while traveling south to north and vice versa for meetings of the Continental Congress. This included Thomas Jefferson, James Madison, John Marshall, and George Mason (all of whom have houses in Virginia with National Historic Landmark status, all of which are included in this book). John Paul Jones,

first commander of the American Navy, came too. After the Battle of Yorktown, which effectively ended the fighting of the American Revolution, Washington held a reception called a Peace Ball here in celebration.

Perhaps due to its reputation as a gathering place, and for its association to the Washington family, the next owner of the house, John Fraser, turned the house into a tavern, which is how the building is interpreted today. During this phase of the building's life, a deep and long porch was added across the whole facade of the building, with the roofline extending outward over the porch, creating a sheltered space for sitting outside, likely welcome during Virginia's hot and humid summers. From 1792 until the mid-19th century, the tavern was in operation, but by this time Americans had woken up to the realization that historic sites associated to the Founding Fathers needed to be preserved, or otherwise would fall into disrepair and eventual destruction. George Washington's home, Mount Vernon, was the first historic house to be saved in such a way, and it influenced others to do the same. In 1907 the tavern was purchased by Preservation Virginia, the organization that manages multiple historic sites across Virginia (including the Cape Henry Lighthouse, Bacon's Castle, and Patrick Henry's Scotchtown, all in this book).

In 2013 a new organization focused directly on Fredericksburg, the Washington Heritage Museums, took over management of the Rising Sun Tavern. Costumed interpreters offer tours seven days a week, and tavern life is stressed, including

discussion of cultural and political life in the late 18th century. The building originally had an attached ballroom (called an assembly room for dancing), which burned
down, and the porch is a re-creation of the original, but the majority of the interior woodwork is original, including balustrades, cornices, a paneled fireplace, and a
built-in cupboard (colonials were fond of built-in cupboards and chests of drawers,
because rooms did not have closets).

Scenic view of the Shenandoah Valley from Skyline Drive, see entry on p. 149.

SHENANDOAH VALLEY

Cedar Creek Battlefield and Belle Grove Plantation
336 Belle Grove Rd., Middletown; (540) 869-2028; bellegrove.org; guided tours of the manor house, Apr through Dec

Battlefield grounds; nps.gov/cebe; open all day every day for driving/ walking/viewing

Listed as one National Historic Landmark but spread over two counties (Frederick and Warren), Cedar Creek Battlefield and Belle Grove Plantation, two sites with distinguished 18th- and 19th-century histories, make an unusual pairing. Taken together, both are part of a National Historical Park, but on its own, Belle Grove is owned by the National Trust for Historic Preservation, while Belle Grove, Inc., a not-for-profit, manages the site and raises funds for continuing preservation work. Likewise, Cedar Creek Battlefield, managed by the National Park Service, also has a partner in the Cedar Creek Battlefield Foundation, another not-for-profit organization. The two sites were incorporated into a single National Historical Park in 2002, with assets and resources still under construction today. Talk about an unusual administrative history!

The fertile area of the Shenandoah Valley is remembered for the 18th century "Age of Grain," when the area became a "breadbasket" for the wheat grown there which made high-quality flour. Additionally, the historic Native American trails and early roads through the Shenandoah Valley were a major thoroughfare connecting the west and southern cities to the north. In the 18th and 19th centuries, the Shenandoah Valley was of great consequence, and by the time of the Civil War, it became even more so and was fought over by Union and Confederate troops for four years.

Belle Grove is part of the National Historical Park due to its survival as one of the most intact 18th-century plantation houses of the Shenandoah Valley. Today the historic site teaches visitors about the intertwined early American heritages of agriculture and plantation life, architecture and the decorative arts, and historic preservation. The original 7,500-acre Belle Grove plantation was owned by Major Isaac

Hite, whose first wife was Nellie Conway Madison, the sister of President James Madison. The status of the Hites is noted in the elegant Jeffersonian architecture of their mansion, which has a symmetrical facade and Palladian window over the portico. Outside the house proper, visitors can do a self-guided tour of the historic landscape, visiting working agricultural fields, a smokehouse and blacksmith shop, barn buildings, and a cemetery with unmarked rough-hewn markers but believed to be for the enslaved who labored here.

Moving on from Belle Grove Plantation—which sits in the middle of the Cedar Creek Battlefield area—head toward the visitor center (7712 Main Street [US 11], Middletown; 504-869-3051). There is also a secondary visitor center at Hupp's Hill operated by the Cedar Creek Battlefield Foundation (www.ccbf.us). After picking up a map at the visitor center and looking at the introductory exhibits, drive the Cedar Creek Battlefield area—which is, in fact, all around the small towns you'll be driving through—stopping at monuments and waysides along the route, which tell the story of the final battle between Union General Philip Sheridan and Confederate General Jubal Early in October 1864. The Union Army burned the Shenandoah Valley, leaving the Confederates and Virginia families without sustenance. Six months later the Confederate Army surrendered at Appomattox.

Cyrus McCormick Farm and Workshop

128 McCormick Farm Cir., Raphine; (540) 377-2255; arec.vaes .vt.edu/arec/shenandoah-valley.html; open daily 8 a.m. to 5 p.m., weather permitting; free admission

At age 22, Cyrus McCormick demonstrated the world's first successful mechanical reaper, working the field in front of his friends and neighbors near his farm, Walnut Grove, in the Shenandoah Valley. It was 1831, and McCormick's invention would change agriculture both in the US and around the world. The machine—a version of which can be seen here at the Cyrus McCormick Farm and Workshop—was strapped to a horse with rider who pulled the contraption forward, while another man walked alongside. This new machine, based on earlier attempts created by his father Robert, harvested grain five times faster than the traditional method of using manual labor with scythes and sickles.

Today Cyrus McCormick, called the Father of Modern Agriculture, might be very pleased to see that his home and workshop are part of Virginia Polytechnic Institute and State University's (Virginia Tech) Shenandoah Valley Agricultural Research and Extension Center. The National Historic Landmark is one of a series of centers around the state conducting research and offering public programs through the Virginia Cooperative Extension program. Researchers and scientists

continue to make contributions to the field, including work done on cattle breeding, nutrition, reproduction, and integrated pest management systems.

Although a working agricultural research facility, visitors can tour the blacksmith shop, gristmill, museum, and scenic sites at the McCormick Farm. When walking in this area you'll also come across McCormick's headstone, because he is buried under a stand of pine trees close to the timber-framed buildings. In addition, there is a lovely trail walk that starts at the workshop buildings and takes visitors into a forested area with nature interpretive panels. The walk parallels a pond teeming with insect life and circles at its end to create a loop.

While walking on the trail there is ample time to think about McCormick's invention and its worldwide significance, which is part of the Industrial Revolution. As Virginia Tech points out in its literature, although the "Virginia Reaper" enabled Americans to produce more food and sustain more healthy people, at the same time fewer people were needed to work on farms, thus precipitating a separation between humans and their food. This transformed, and inverted, American society and culture: Before the mechanization of agriculture in the 19th century, 90 percent of Americans worked the land. Today, fewer than 2 percent do, and the closure of family farms continues well into the 21st century.

McCormick patented his invention in 1834, but went on to continue innovating in agriculture by introducing new ideas to help farmers. By integrating business techniques into agriculture, he helped the US become the standard-bearer of food production. At first farmers were slow to adopt his ideas, but eventually his business grew so large—he was actually crafting the Virginia Reapers in his blacksmith shop on-site—that the company went west, where farmers were sowing large tracts of new farmland. And, in a perfect expression of the value the Western world placed on McCormick's invention, at the famous 1850 Crystal Palace exhibition in London, the Virginia Reaper won the gold medal. America had beaten England—a country that had been farming for more than a millennia.

Natural Bridge State Park
6477 South Lee Hwy., Natural Bridge; (540) 291-1326; dcr.virginia .gov/state-parks/natural-bridge#general_information; open daily 9 a.m. to 5 p.m. with special programs; admission charged

Along the eastern edge of the Blue Ridge Mountains, an extremely long mountain crest that runs from just north of the Potomac River on the Virginia–Maryland border south all the way to northern Georgia, is found a limestone arch carved out of water millions of years ago. This tall, narrow passage (you can both walk underneath it or drive over it) was, for Thomas Jefferson, a place that drew his great admiration—even passion—for more than five decades. The Natural Bridge, as of 2016, is a site of the Virginia State Park system, but it has been many more things: sacred landscape for the Monacan Indians; edge of the wilderness for the young US; tourist site during the Victorian era; tourist site again in the 20th century, when motels, wax museums, and other roadside tourist attractions were in vogue; and even today the site of biblical storytelling from an evangelical viewpoint. Due to the historic site's changeover from private to public hands, the Natural Bridge now has the opportunity to refocus on the environmental and historic aspects of the landscape, introducing new generations of fans to a landscape feature seemingly more common to the Southwest than to the East.

The Natural Bridge is a limestone arch over Cedar Creek that stands 215 miles high and 90 feet long. It has been an admired natural wonder since the 18th century, not only in the US but also in Europe. According to legend, George Washington surveyed the bridge and cut his initials into one of the interior walls. Thomas Jefferson was so enthralled by the Natural Bridge that he purchased it and 157 surrounding acres from the Crown in 1774. He wrote several times about the arch, not surprisingly, most thoroughly in his book, *Notes on the State of Virginia*. According to Jefferson, standing on the bridge and looking down at the river below, "You voluntarily fall on your hands and feet, creep to the parapet, and peep over it." Jefferson visited Natural Bridge at least six times between 1773 and 1821. He first saw the Natural Bridge in 1767 with the help of a guide, as it was located at the edge of civilization where the "West" began, and drew a diagram of it on the flyleaf of his "Farm Book."

It's important to remember that when Jefferson and others traveled to see the Natural Bridge, there was no hotel waiting with warm beds and warm food as there is today.

The Natural Bridge State Park consists of 1,540 acres in Rockbridge County 3 miles off of I-81, at Routes 11 and 130. On-site are a gift shop, food services, and the Natural Bridge Historic Hotel & Conference Center—once called a "grand lady" with 118 guest rooms, a full-service dining room, a tavern and a meeting space. In addition there are walking trails and special programs throughout the year such as carriage rides and luminary nights.

Skyline Drive

**Shenandoah National Park, Luray; nps.gov/shen/planyourvisit/
driving-skyline-drive.htm; open every day except during inclement
weather; admission $25 per car**

The Blue Ridge Mountains, which stretch from Pennsylvania to North Carolina, are
a nature and history lovers' paradise. Seen from vantage points across Central Virginia and the Shenandoah Valley, the mountains are accessible via hiking trails (the
Appalachian Trail traverses the Blue Ridge) but, in a way that only Americans could
dream up, the mountains are accessible by car along Skyline Drive, a magnificent feat
of architectural engineering. Built of concrete in the 1930s when the federal government dreamt big and provided capital improvement jobs for thousands of Americans
during the Great Depression, Skyline Drive runs 105 miles north and south along
the crest of the Blue Ridge Mountains in Shenandoah National Park and is the only
public road through the park. It takes about three hours to travel the entire length of
the park on a clear day. You can enter Shenandoah at only four places: Front Royal
Entrance Station near Route 66 and 340; Thornton Gap Entrance Station at Route
211; Swift Run Gap Entrance Station at Route 33; Rockfish Gap Entrance Station
at Route 64 and Rt. 250

Although you could do Skyline Drive in a matter of hours, the parkway road
is a platform for explorations as you head north (or south, depending). Parkway
pull-offs for viewing rolling waves of green mountains are frequent—and, often, so
are black bear sightings! (I once picked up a jogger who wanted to avoid a black
bear having a good time trying to eat bugs in a tree stump). Numerous trails, in

addition to the Appalachian Trail, provide different grades of access in and around the craggy ridge. Skyline Drive belongs to the age of belief in the benefits of automobiles and the pleasure they produce, but also in the tourism opportunities presented to local communities. Along Skyline Drive you'll find campgrounds and picnic areas if that is your preferred mode, or, at Skyland Resort and Big Meadows, in the heart of Shenandoah National Park, there are lodges, restaurants, gift shops, and camp stores. During the warm weather months, outdoor concerts, guided nature walks, and festivals (to the blackberry—a bear's favorite treat!) are on the books, as are night hikes to view the starry skies.

A magical journey on Skyline Drive doesn't really have to end. If you reach the southern access point at mile marker 105.4, you can turn off and drive down the mountain to Thomas Jefferson's city, Charlottesville, or keep going. The terminus of Skyline Drive connects directly to the Blue Ridge Parkway, "America's Favorite Journey" another two-lane parkway connecting Virginia to the Great Smoky Mountains in Tennessee. At night, Skyline Drive is open, but there are absolutely no lights, so, extra precaution must be taken on the windy roads. The speed limit is 35 and should be obeyed—park police are watching, although the steep cliffs and lack of guardrails in many places suggest safe driving all on their own. Franklin Delano Roosevelt gave the dedication speech for the opening of Shenandoah National Park (and Skyline Drive within it) on July 3, 1936, but it was the culmination of work first put forward by another US president, Herbert Hoover, 10 years earlier.

Stonewall Jackson's Headquarters
415 N. Braddock St., Winchester; (540) 667-5505; winchester history.org/stonewall-jacksons-headquarters; open Apr through Oct, Mon through Sat 10 a.m. to 4 p.m., Sun noon to 4 p.m.; admission charged

Here you are in Winchester, the northernmost city in the Shenandoah Valley in Virginia (Harper's Ferry, Charlestown, and Martinsburg, now all in West Virginia, were part of Virginia until splitting from the state during the Civil War). Once you get to know a little about Virginia history, so thoroughly steeped in the FFF (First Founding Families), the American Revolution, and the Confederacy, it comes as no surprise that the first National Historic Landmark to be seen in the Shenandoah Valley is associated with Thomas "Stonewall" Jackson. For more than 125 years, Jackson was a beloved hero to Virginians. His house is preserved and re-created in Lexington; there are bronze monuments to him across the Commonwealth, including an equestrian on Monument Avenue in Richmond and a bronze standing in front of the formal entry at the Virginia Military Institute. His gravesite in Lexington still attracts visitors, and even in Lynchburg there are the rotted-out remnants of the packet boat *Marshall* still on display in Riverside Park. The boat carried his body from Lynchburg to Lexington after his untimely death in 1863. He was accidentally shot by Confederate troops from North Carolina at the Battle of Chancellorsville.

General Thomas Jackson was a graduate of West Point who had earlier fought in the Mexican War (1846–1848) and then taught for 10 years at the Virginia Military

Institute in Lexington. He earned the name Stonewall at the First Battle of Manassas in 1861 for his steadfast stance on the battlefield—he was said to be as strong and unmoving as a stone wall.

Jackson used this house in Winchester for just over a year from 1861 to 1862, designing his Shenandoah Valley campaigns from the Gothic Revival cottage. The success of his campaign, in which Jackson beat the Union Army, earned him respect across the Confederate Army and South and a legacy that was revived long after the end of the war. The small house—designed in a Gothic Revival style common in the mid-19th century—was turned over for Jackson's use by Lt. Colonial Lewis T. Moore, whose descendant, television icon Mary Tyler Moore, helped restore the home 100 years later. The cottage has details that are more characteristic to the Hudson Valley in New York, versus the Shenandoah Valley, including Gothic pointed windows and Carpenter Gothic trim under the roofline. Jackson and his wife were happy in Winchester and thought to return to the town when the war ended. Of course, fate had something different in store for Jackson, but this house is filled with memorabilia and artifacts once belonging to him and about the Civil War. Winchester makes a good starting point for a tour of Shenandoah Valley battlefields and Civil War historic sites, but it's also a way into seeing firsthand how Virginians constructed memory around losing the Civil War.

Thunderbird Archaeological District
Limeton; private property

The only prehistoric indigenous site on the National Historic Landmark registry in Virginia is the Thunderbird Archaeological District. Almost unheard of outside of archaeology circles, Thunderbird is located near Front Royal, the northernmost entrance to Skyline Drive and Shenandoah National Park. Front Royal is a busy town during the warm weather season. In addition to Shenandoah, there are caverns to visit (Shenandoah and Luray), state parks, and family-friendly attractions. Because Thunderbird no longer has a dedicated visitor center nor trail marker, its history has been forgotten. But, 40 years ago, during the 1970s, the site—expanding across more than 2,000 acres—was a hotbed of archaeological activity. Universities, students, and volunteers identified and excavated the site, uncovering thousands of stone tools, and even the remains of what is considered one of the oldest structures in North America. One of the sites, called "Thunderbird" by Dr. William Gardner of the Catholic University of America, became shorthand for the whole district. Gardner, with the support of John D. Flynn Jr., who owned most of the land, opened a museum and visitor center to tell what was thought to be a developing story to the public and to display their work. Little did they know what was in store for Thunderbird.

The research established Thunderbird—with its complex of prehistoric and historic sites—as one of the oldest archaeological sites in North America. The periods of habitation and use date from the Paleo-Indian (9500 B.C.E.) through the Late Woodland (1600 C.E.) periods. Several stratified Paleo-Indian sites were investigated, and some of the Western Hemisphere's earliest evidence of structures was discovered. The project, one of America's few fully documented Paleo-Indian settlement patterns, led to the development of chronological sequences for the Shenandoah Valley with ramifications for eastern North American regions in general. Two sites within the district, the Thunderbird Site and Site Fifty, were named National Historic Landmarks within the Thunderbird Archaeological District.

Thunderbird was given National Historic Landmark status because of the rich, long, layered settlement patterns dating back 12,000 years—the time when the earliest men and women migrated to, and settled in, North America. Evidence for these early lives was found just below the plowline and were therefore undisturbed. Successive layers were intact, yielding the material culture left behind by these indigenous people, who became the ancestors of today's Native American cultures. The site yielded significant and unique projectile points—especially in jasper—but also discolorations in the soil, called postholes, where wood posts, used to construct buildings, left behind traces. Specific archaeological sites within the district were unusually untouched by time, because the nearby Flint River had flooded and covered the area many times over, acting as a protective layer.

Sadly, the owner of the land and the head archaeologist lost control of the property due to lack of money, and the land was purchased and divided by developers. The museum was closed. Today, "Keep Out/Private Road" signs dot the area. It is important to remember Thunderbird, and include it in this book, because history consists not only of things built aboveground, but also ancient history below our feet. It is best to not try and visit the district, but instead to read more about the indigenous people who came to settle what we today called Virginia—they were here for more than 10,000 years before Europeans. For further reading and images, see Helen C. Roundtree's *Pocahontas's People: The Powhatan Indians of Virginia through Four Centuries* (University of Oklahoma Press, 1990) and Keith Egloff's *First People: The Early Indians of Virginia* (University of Virginia Press, 1992).

Virginia Military Institute Historic District
VMI Parade Grounds, 319 Letcher Ave., Lexington; (540) 464-7211; vmi.edu/admissions-and-aid/visit

Twelve of the Virginia Military Institute's 200 acres in the Shenandoah Valley were designated a National Historic Landmark District in 1974. Called VMI in shorthand, cadets from across the nation come here to attend college and learn

leadership skills, which may be continued in the armed forces (cadets are members of the ROTC) or applied to their future civilian work. Founded in 1839, VMI is the nation's oldest state-supported military college. A day spent in historic Lexington must include a visit to VMI: The school's 19th- and 20th-century architecture, centered around the green parade field, is a unique experience. Students live in austere conditions "on Post" (which means "on campus"), under a strict military lifestyle. The cadets are a pleasure to talk to—especially the women, who finally gained access to this institute of higher learning in 1997. Although still a small percentage of the student body (11 percent are female, compared to the 89 percent male student body), VMI is beginning, after more than two decades, to look more like 21st-century America.

Famous Americans have attended VMI. From the military perspective, George S. Patton and George C. Marshall are iconic figures. But, surprisingly, there have been a handful of celebrities, too, including comedians/actors Fred Willard and Mel Brooks (who would have guessed?). Beyond walking the grounds of the pre-famous, on campus there are multiple sites and buildings to visit, including the George C. Marshall Museum and Library (Tues through Sat, 11 a.m. to 4 p.m., entrance fee), as well as the Jackson Memorial Hall and Preston Library, which contains the VMI Museum (free—see the mounted hide of "Little Sorrel," Stonewall Jackson's horse). Most Friday afternoons when school is in session, VMI cadets parade in full dress uniform—an opportunity that the public and visitors can watch freely. In addition, cadet-guided tours are offered at noon for free during the school year, which start at the VMI Museum.

VMI began as a step up from a local militia and armory installation and was rather poor and underfunded until the mid-19th century. New barracks were built and faculty attracted new faces, such as Thomas "Stonewall" Jackson, who came to VMI to teach in 1851. When the Civil War broke out, students went in different directions—some became Union infantry and one became an officer, but, not surprisingly, hundreds of VMI cadets and alumni became Confederate soldiers, 15 became generals, and more were division commanders, brigadiers, and colonels. One VMI graduate and Confederate, Moses Ezekiel, became a sculptor. You can see his work in the monument *Virginia Mourning Her Dead* on campus. Ezekiel also

designed the Thomas Jefferson Monument in front of the Rotunda at the University of Virginia (also pictured in this book). He was the first Jewish graduate of the school in 1866 and fought at the Battle of New Market in the Shenandoah Valley.

Barracks, Virginia Military Institute
VMI Parade Grounds, 319 Letcher Ave., Lexington; (540) 464-7211; vmi.edu/admissions-and-aid/visit

Thanks to the Commonwealth's early history tied to England, and to Thomas Jefferson, Virginia is a state covered in Neoclassical architecture, the preferred style of the 18th century across the Atlantic world. There are only a few examples of historic buildings on the National Historic Landmark register in Virginia built in a differing architectural style, and the Barracks is a particularly fine example. By the first half of the 19th century, architect Alexander Jackson Davis had found fame—and a lot of work—when Americans became attracted to the Gothic Revival, which held different connotations in architecture, as compared to the Neoclassical. While Gothic Revival was often thought appropriate for ecclesiastical buildings such as churches, the Gothic—dating from the Middle Ages—was also a good fit for military uses, because it brings forward historical images of fortified castles and keeps and towers with crenellation. The "Old" Barrack at VMI, the only survivor of a larger group of

buildings, is an example of this interest in the Gothic Revival, which features a central "tower" or block and crenellation along its roofline.

Facing the parade grounds, the Barracks forms a protective barrier and also a stunning backdrop for the weekly parade exercises. Visitors today cannot enter the Barracks, because it is still used as a residence hall for VMI cadets. But you can walk around the 500-foot-long exterior of the building as well as the parade grounds, viewing all of the buildings, which include the homes of VMI senior administrators and the George C. Marshall Museum. Bronze monuments and tablets can be seen, and the walk also includes a stop at the VMI Museum. Thomas "Stonewall" Jackson would have used this building, since its original construction date precedes his arrival on campus by just a few years. His bronze monument stands at the exterior entryway, surrounded by brightly painted red cannon. Traces of Stonewall Jackson can be seen throughout Lexington: Close by in the VMI Museum, but also his gravesite and house are both a 20-minute walk into town. The house has been re-created to imagine Jackson's life while he was teaching at VMI.

The "Old" Barracks is the oldest surviving building on campus, but its Gothic Revival design became the style for all of the VMI campus, and later architects, such as Bertram Grosvenor Goodhue, would continue building in this style. Behind the parade grounds is the sports stadium—built yet again, in the iconic style of the Gothic. Perhaps the founding father of VMI had something to do with choosing this style as well—Col. Claude Crozet, ousted from the French military for which he served under Napoleon, helped to found the school and served as its first president. Modeling VMI after West Point, which also utilized Gothic Revival architecture, Crozet would have been very familiar and comfortable with the Gothic style. The Gothic is a French invention from the Middle Ages!

Washington and Lee University Historic District
204 W. Washington St., Lexington; (540) 458-8400; wlu.edu/
about-wandl/visiting-wandl; campus open to visitors

In 1972 the historic core of Washington and Lee University was designated a National Historic Landmark District—it was only the third campus in the country to be given such status and is the ninth-oldest institution of higher learning in the country. Washington and Lee, usually abbreviated to W&L, is named for two Virginians, both of whom had ties to this historic school located in the Shenandoah Valley. George Washington was a benefactor of the college (the school was renamed Washington College for him)—and he still stands on the pinnacle of Washington Hall, in the center of the Colonnade, which is the most striking feature of the W&L campus. This building contains a lobby space with exhibits and materials on and

about George Washington and the connections of the earliest W&L staff in using the ideal figure of Washington to teach students moral codes of conduct.

This area of the historic campus looking across to Lee Chapel comprises the three oldest buildings, but as a series of buildings that can be walked, there are five in a row. Washington Hall, Robinson Hall, Payne Hall, Newcomb Hall, and Tucker

Hall are all fronted with two-story high porticos (covered walkways with columns). Walking this impressive Colonnade, on bricks that are almost 200 years old, you can see traces of the past. Each doorway has a well-worn stoop, and many still retain their metal boot cleaners, sitting close to the bottom step. Most important to contemplate is the fact that these bricks were made by enslaved people, some of whom were inherited by the school when trustee John Robinson gave his 400-acre farm, livestock, whiskey distillery, and 73 enslaved men, women, and children to it in 1826. This was intended to boost the financial

stability of the college, because Robinson stipulated that these material things could be sold to assist the precarious economics of the school, which had only 65 students and no endowment.

Washington College sold off these material goods during the 19th century—including most of the enslaved people. Many were sent to work in cotton fields in Mississippi after being purchased by a Lynchburger, whose name, Samuel S. Garland, became the name of one of the city's historic districts. A stone marker placed on the east side of Robinson Hall at W&L remembers the enslaved people and how monetary value was assigned to their work, and to their bodies. Although three elderly enslaved people were part of Washington College until the Civil War, nothing is known about them after Emancipation. But Washington College was about to take a different direction in the post–Civil War years: General Robert E. Lee, the famed military leader of the Confederate States of America, and a Virginian, came to the school to teach and live out his remaining years. Only a year after his death in 1870, the school changed its name to Washington and Lee University.

What makes W&L different from other early American colleges is its location in Lexington and the development of the Lost Cause narrative, which can be examined closely by visiting the Lee Chapel and Museum (entrance to the museum located under the chapel).

Lee Chapel

Washington and Lee University, Lexington; (540) 458-8786; lee chapel.wlu.edu; open Apr 1 through Oct 1 Mon through Sat 9 a.m. to 5 p.m., Sun 1 p.m. to 5 p.m. and Nov 1 through Mar 31 Mon through Sat 9 a.m. to 5 p.m., Sun 1 p.m. to 4 p.m.; tours daily; free

Part of the Washington and Lee National Historic Landmark District is an individual building with its own National Historic Landmark listing—Lee Chapel, built in 1866 for campus prayer and gatherings. After Robert E. Lee's death, the building became Lee's final resting place and, for this reason, has since become a tourist attraction. Today, in the 21st century, Washington and Lee University is again rethinking this status, since inside the chapel the marble statue of the deceased Lee lies behind the altar, elevating a man whom many admire, but many more revile as a symbol of the difficult and disturbing history of enslavement and the Confederacy itself. Until very recently Lee's tomb was surrounded by Confederate battle flags. The town of Lexington recently removed these flags from their downtown streetscape. W&L followed suit due to the flag's continuing notoriety. In August 2017, for example, Confederate battle flags were used by participants in the Unite the Right rally on the campus of the University of Virginia.

It would be easy to talk around these hard issues and present information on the Victorian-era architecture and the collections housed below within the W&L Museum. But Robert E. Lee isn't just any Virginian, and W&L isn't just any college. In the 21st century we now see this history and heritage through different eyes. After the war Lee needed a place to go. He was the leader of the defeated rebels who had tried to secede from the Union, and the federal government had seized his house and land (eventually becoming Arlington National Cemetery). Offered a position at

W&L, Lee accepted, and he's known to have helped rejuvenate the school by offering practical education within the liberal arts curriculum, transforming the sleepy Southern school into a modern institution. It was Lee who saw the need to build a chapel, and when he died only five years later, he was interred there.

The chapel served the campus environment until the early 1960s, when National Historic Landmark status was given to the building, and a renovation turning the structure into a professional museum took place. Lee's marble statue—recumbent, hands folded over chest—is just that, a statue. His remains, and that of his wife, seven children, and other Lee family descendants, are all interred below in the crypt. And in a way this really speaks to a mix of military traditions, the Victorian era, and the South, as Lee's famous horse Traveller is also buried close by—right outside the doors to the museum so that he could be close to Lee. If you walk around the historic district of the W&L campus, you will see a redbrick house and, at the back, two large green-painted garage doors. This building belongs to the president of the university, but the doors always stay open, because this is where Traveller once lived when the garage was a stable, and it's believed the spirit of the horse needs to be able to roam freely!

Woodrow Wilson Birthplace (The Woodrow Wilson Presidential Library and Museum)
20 N. Coalter St., Staunton; (540) 885-0897; woodrowwilson.org; variety of tours offered year-round; admission charged

Woodrow Wilson's birthplace, known as the Presbyterian Manse, is an antebellum house on the west side of the Blue Ridge Mountains. It is one of three presidential homes in Virginia that is also a presidential library and museum. Wilson is known today as the president who brought the US into World War I and also for being so ill while in office his wife, Edith Bolling Wilson, became his virtual stand-in. Because he lived during a tumultuous moment in American history—the first world war of the 20th century, the Spanish flu epidemic, suffrage, and Prohibition for starters—Wilson is a fascinating, though difficult, Virginian to study. This is because Wilson deployed racial segregationist policies, called Jim Crow, in his administration, erasing gains made by African Americans after the Civil War.

Since most Americans think of Virginia as the home to many of the Founding Fathers, Wilson has been forgotten as a Virginian president. Visiting this National Historic Landmark site goes far in placing Wilson in the context of where and when he was born: 1856, to be exact, in this house, which was given to his father, the Rev. Joseph Ruggles Wilson, a Presbyterian minister. Wilson, born Thomas Woodrow Wilson and therefore known as Tommy as a youth, later lived in Georgia and South

Carolina, as his father was transferred. Wilson graduated from Princeton (like another Virginian president, James Madison), received a law degree, and then a PhD from Johns Hopkins University. Learning—not the law—was his true love. Entering the teaching profession, Wilson excelled, eventually becoming the president of Princeton University and then governor of New Jersey. Two years later, in 1912, Wilson was elected president of the US.

Wilson did enact several pieces of legislation that alleviated social ills for Americans, including the Child Labor Reform Act. And out of the tumult of World War I and the changing borders and political leadership, Wilson created the idea of a League of Nations, in addition to his famous "Fourteen Points of Light" for the Treaty of Versailles. Neither was adopted or enacted by the US, and the harsh conditions placed on Germany are now considered to have created conditions for the rise of National Socialism (the Nazi party). Wilson wouldn't live long enough to witness the Great Depression or World War II. He died in 1924 after having a stroke while in office.

The museum has several interesting features, including a 1919 Pierce–Arrow limousine (a presidential car Wilson loved so much, it was purchased for him by friends after he left office) and a re-created trench of the Western front. Changing exhibits introduce visitors to Wilson's era and to the many ways in which his policies and leadership shaped society. There are gardens to tour, a presidential library to visit if you want to do research, and collections that support the many stories of Wilson's life and legacy.

Thomas Jefferson's Poplar Forest, see entry on p. 169

VIRGINIA MOUNTAINS

The Homestead (The Omni Homestead Resort)
**7696 Sam Snead Hwy., Hot Springs; (800) 838-1766; omnihotels
.com/hotels/homestead-virginia; visitors welcome year-round**

One of the farthest National Historic Landmarks in the western part of Virginia, and the only resort to have such designation, is the Omni Homestead, nestled in the Allegheny Mountains. If you are traveling from the east, the drive to the Omni Homestead is spectacular—up and over the Blue Ridge Mountains, through the Shenandoah Valley, to the Alleghenies, much of which is forested land (the Washington and Jefferson National Forest, to be exact). This place has attracted visitors for more than 200 years, who come to recreate and relax, but also, most wonderfully, to visit the last operational springs, a therapeutic activity called hydrotherapy, where people bathe in the springs that range from cold to hot.

Although a commercial enterprise, the Omni Homestead is packed with local and national history. Long before the construction of large banqueting and accommodation facilities, the area drew those attracted to "taking the waters," a practice in

existence in Europe since the ancient era, but continuing right up until the modern age. Americans would also do this; the most famous visitor to the hot springs in Bath County was Thomas Jefferson, who came in 1818. Like many mature adults, Jefferson suffered from rheumatism, headaches, and other ailments that grew worse as he grew older. Traveling over the mountains by horse, Jefferson stayed for two weeks in Hot Springs—a scene which is painted in a mural located inside the Omni Homestead hotel today.

Beyond "taking the waters," visitors come to the resort to utilize some of the 2,000 acres of land for hiking, horseback riding, and, in the winter, skiing. In addition, there are zip lines, tennis courts, a water park, swimming pools, and two golf courses associated to the resort. But all of these activities happen around the centerpiece of the property: the hotel itself, which is mammoth. There are 438 guest rooms and multiple restaurants and shops. The Omni Homestead is really a village unto itself, but its history can be found when looking at a series of prints by Edward Beyer in the hallways, titled "Album of Virginia," or when you have a drink at the bar just off the lobby, where presidential portraits hang neatly in rows. American presidents have, in fact, been a large part of the Omni Homestead's history—William Howard Taft visited, as did Theodore Roosevelt. Both men, part of the Gilded Age, likely came to stay in the new resort building, erected in 1901 and 1902 after the original structures burned down. Financier J. P. Morgan was behind this investment, and illustrations of the Gilded Age and its sporting culture are depicted in the murals.

The Omni Homestead changed ownership and names several times at the end of the 20th century, and today it is a part of the National Trust for Historic Preservation Program, Historic Hotels of America. Although there is plenty to do at the Homestead, my favorite activity is free and easy: Have a sit on the huge front porch that extends the length of the facade and watch visitors come and go!

Humpback Bridge
Rte. 60, Midland Trail, Covington

What is it about a covered bridge that makes people so happy? Scenes from Currier and Ives from the 19th century show covered bridges in wintertime, or in fall, with the leaves' brightly changing colors. Since that time, covered bridges remain a cherished part of the American landscape in the eastern half of the country. Virginia has only 7 covered bridges remaining, out of more than 100 that originally existed before the arrival of the automobile. Out of these 7, only 4 can be visited (and walked on—the remaining 3 are on private property). Humpback Bridge is special, though. It is the oldest of the last 7 covered bridges in Virginia, and it has, well, a humpback!

Built in 1857, Humpback Bridge spans 109 feet across Dunlap Creek, with its middle section raised 4 feet higher than its ends. The wooden bridge was used until

1929, when a steel bridge was built for the developing roadways for cars. Covered bridges developed out of earlier simple wooden bridges, as it was believed that the covering would protect the wood underneath and help the bridge last longer (which, in fact, turned out to be true). Hardy woods such as hickory and white oak were used, but, even then, the effects of sunlight and moisture—of which Virginia has plenty in the Shenandoah Valley—meant a shortened life span. Humpback Bridge has had elements replaced over time, but the hand-hewn support timbers and decking are original, attesting to the materials, craftsmanship, and decision to cover the bridge.

All of the remaining covered bridges in Virginia are on the western side of the state, indicating the importance of bridges as access routes for farmers transporting their goods from the Shenandoah Valley up and over the Alleghenies farther west. Although known later as "kissing bridges," because a covered bridge would shield couples from prying eyes, the practicality of a covered bridge shouldn't be forgotten. Today a small green area, called the Humpback Bridge Wayside Park, purchased when the bridge was listed on the historic register, serves as a rest area with picnic tables and restroom facilities. The park is one of the most favored photo-friendly sites for taking your own #LOVEVA pictures with the Humpback Bridge as your own Currier and Ives backdrop!

Thomas Jefferson's Poplar Forest
1542 Bateman Bridge Rd., Forest; (434) 525-1806; poplarforest .org; open year-round except major holidays, many special events; admission charged

Few people know how keenly Thomas Jefferson valued intimate, quiet time with his family. Recognized for his wide breadth of interests covering architecture, agriculture, philosophy, medicine, horticulture, and more, Americans generally assign a few big events in history to Jefferson—his writing of the Declaration of Independence, serving as third president, and, finally, his coordination of the Louisiana Purchase and exploration of the West by Lewis and Clark.

Today Americans also recognize that Jefferson, like many of the Founding Fathers and presidents, was also a slave owner, although his relationship to the enslaved community living around him was closer than most, as he fathered children with Sally Hemings, a young enslaved woman—directly related to his wife Martha—who worked in his house. Thomas Jefferson is a complicated character with many layers to peel back, but this house, called Poplar Forest for the plantation he inherited when he married in 1771, is clear and direct: The house is a perfect octagon, built in what was once a rural area of Virginia, far from the hustle and bustle of busy Monticello and Charlottesville.

Here at Poplar Forest, in a brick house designed with large glass windows and one of the first skylights created for an American home, Jefferson stayed—often two, three, or four times a year—with his granddaughters and always accompanied on

the three-day journey from Monticello by his enslaved manservant, Burwell Colbert. Although Poplar Forest is an exquisite house, a building designed, in the words of Jefferson, "for the faculties of a private citizen," its use was of great value to his personal economy; the Poplar Forest plantation offered 5,000 acres of land for growing the cash crops that were his bread and butter, namely wheat, tobacco, and vegetables. Although Jefferson owned the land for three decades previous, he only began building his octagon house in 1806, desiring a retreat where he could "indulge in the life of the mind and renew his personal creativity."

Jefferson's Poplar Forest was listed as a National Historic Landmark in 1969 while the house was still under private ownership. In the 1980s a group of local citizens banded together to save the house and purchase tracts of land around it that were originally part of the plantation. Today 619 acres are intact, encompassing fields, creeks, a pond, and a stand of poplar trees in front of the house, which date from Jefferson's era. The house continues to undergo interior restoration, but it's open for tours. The grounds around the house itself are also undergoing restoration with new clumps of trees and plantings taking hold as well as a new carriage turnaround, discovered after overgrown boxwood bushes were removed and archaeologists dug into the soil.

There is only one American president who designed two spectacular homes for himself, both of which survive and are open for visitors. Poplar Forest is precious in that it offers a private view of a very public man.

CONCLUSION

It's true that the National Historic Landmarks Program, as it currently exists in Virginia, is very much representative of the 20th century—both in the choices made for site selection, nomination, and registration and in the content presented in these landmarks. Since that time, history "written from below" (that is, from perspectives other than the white elites at the top of society) and a renewed dedication to equity and equality have changed what subject matter is of interest to historians today and the way it is written, presented, and codified in such historic registers. The National Historic Landmarks which I've selected and described in this book aren't less important than before, but, their interpretation has changed, and each will be joined by new landmarks that balance out the selections that already exist. The challenge for the National Historic Landmarks Program is the criteria on which successful nominations rest: properties need to have historic integrity; therefore, for early cultures such as indigenous populations of Virginia, or for marginalized populations such as enslaved African Americans, sometimes little in the way of material culture in built form survives.

The National Park Service, which manages the National Historic Landmarks program, recognizes these challenges and the work ahead. Toward this end, they have created at least four new initiatives since 2011—the American Latino Heritage Initiative, the Asian American and Pacific Islander Heritage Initiative, the Lesbian, Gay, Bisexual, Transgender, and Queer (LGBTQ) Heritage Initiative, and the Women's History Initiative—with the goal of furthering the representation of diverse stories within the National Historic Landmarks Program and elsewhere within the National Park Service. According to the National Park Service, "the initiatives are intended to extend the reach of documentation, listing, and designation of historic places to better reflect the full spectrum of people, events, and experiences that have contributed to building the nation." This is something to cheer on, and I'm pleased to think that the next iteration of this book might look very different from this one.

THEMATIC INDEX

PHOTO CREDITS

ACKNOWLEDGMENTS

Thanks to Amy Lyons and Sarah Parke of Globe Pequot for asking me to share my enthusiasm for Virginia and its special places through the lens of the National Historic Landmarks Program. Many thanks to Susan McCall for sharing her love for Williamsburg through her photographs and connections to the many costumed interpreters who make Williamsburg come alive for visitors. Thanks also to Taft Kiser for suggesting books on indigenous people's history in Virginia. Many thanks to each and every person who helped me obtain images and information for this book, including Jeffrey Nichols, Joanna Catron, Kelley Fanto Deetz, and Sarah F. Whiting. Thanks to Al Chambers for sharing a copy of his book *National Landmarks, America's Treasures* with me (in which he wrote a short synopsis of more than 2,200 National Historic Landmarks across the US!). Finally, thanks to Caridad de la Vega, a historian with the National Historic Landmarks Program, who pointed out the ways landmark nominations come into being, the parameters and mission of the program, and the work they do and would like to do more of, if more resources were available.

It is important to acknowledge the National Park Service, the manager of the National Historic Landmarks Program and of many of the historic sites described here. During the writing of this book, the federal government experienced the longest shutdown in American history (35 days). While websites were up and running, they were not updated, nor were any but the most essential staff at work. So-called "nonessential" staff included park rangers, historians, and those working for special programs such as the National Historic Landmarks. These public history frontline folks were not available to scholars for consultation and not available to the public for site visits, tours, or educational programs. National parks, monuments, and historic sites were closed. Many natural and cultural areas were damaged due to lack over oversight and daily maintenance.

I did not foresee this twist when I began to write this book, and it was a sad thing to watch and experience. I live close to, and use regularly, several National Park Service sites, including Shenandoah National Park, the Blue Ridge Parkway, and Appomattox Court House National Historical Park. Not being able to access updated historical information for this project drove home knowledge of the importance of the Department of the Interior and the National Park Service to the US. Americans and visitors are fortunate to have these places to visit, enjoy, and learn from. It is the very nature of a federal program that the historical documentation of each park, landmark, or historic site, completed by professionals over the course of